Spinning the Bottle Again:
Fundamentals and Case Studies in
Wine Public Relations

Paul Franson and Harvey Posert

To Denise, best fans.
One of my
Paul Franson
July 23, 2012

1

Spinning the Bottle Again:
Fundamentals and Case Studies in
Wine Public Relations

Paul Franson and Harvey Posert

A wholly revised and updated successor to *Spinning the Bottle* with contributions from some of the wine industry's leading marketers and other experts. Edited with some chapters contributed by Harvey Posert and Paul Franson.

Preface by Robert Mondavi

HPPR Press

St. Helena, California

2012

ISBN: 978-0-9851392-0-9

Spinning the Bottle Again

Table of Contents

Preface to First Edition of *Spinning The Bottle*

I always knew that Napa Valley had the soils, the climate and the grape varieties to make wines that ranked with the finest in the world. But once we achieved that quality, public relations programs and publicity were crucial in telling the world about our wines and the appropriate place of wine in our lives. We invested large sums in that educational effort, and I know that it played a major role in our success.

I'm pleased to see that Harvey Posert, who led our program for many years, and Paul Franson are publishing this book. In my mind, public relations – after wine quality – remains the most important factor in winery success. The case histories and other information in this book should be helpful to everyone in the wine business.

We always believed that our success depended on the success of the industry and that we should share our knowledge for the good of all of us. *Spinning the Bottle* does just that, and I thank all the contributors.

The late Robert Mondavi

Napa Valley

Winter 2003

An Insider's Perspective:

Introduction by Harvey Posert

This introduction tells the story of my career in wine public relations, which began in 1965. It appears that I was born to do this work, although I never drank wine until college (English majors drank Taylor Dry Sherry), and I never heard of PR until I worked for the PR Director of the American Bar Association while at the University of Chicago Law School. Those of you who know the story can move on to the book.

Thanks to a sports editor uncle, I began writing sports for the Memphis Commercial Appeal at age 14, and thanks to him and another newspapering uncle I worked on the paper for 10 summers during school and after Army Counterintelligence. I filled in for beat reporters during their summer vacations, so I worked on the food, business, agriculture, travel and feature desks at some time.

I left law school and joined the Daniel Edelman PR agency in Chicago, working with consumer products like Sara Lee and Lava Lite, some trade associations and Sargent Shriver, manager of the Merchandise Mart where our office was located. That time and place has been dubbed "The Chicago School" of PR —heavy in product publicity but light on counseling and issues communications.

Returning to Memphis for three years, I operated an agency which handled some products and political campaigns. Then Dan Edelman hired me back to run his NY office, and that gave me major media work and trade association issues experience.

In 1965 Wine Institute initiated a total PR review, firing three agencies which had handled the "premium wine" (Almaden, Paul Masson, Inglenook, Krug), "popular wine" (Gallo, Italian Swiss, Guild) and wine-and-health programs. Of the 60-plus agencies competing, WI hired Harry Serlis from the group and told him to make the selection. Because the "enemies" of wine at that time were believed to be ignorant of wine in general and prejudiced against California wine in particular, Harry chose Dan's firm for our apparent publicity capabilities and our ignorance of the wine business —we didn't know enough to argue. He said then, and I've found it true, that you can teach someone about wine but you can't teach PR judgment and skill and enthusiasm for publicity work.

Dan had made the usual promises —cover of Time, offices we didn't have at the time, etc. —for our largest agency fee of $60,000 a year; Harry wisely raised it to $90,000 but said he wanted it all done. I moved to San Francisco and we put a team together —many are authors in this book —with media and market programs in New York, Chicago, Washington, Los Angeles and San Francisco. We hired traveling wine experts for media calls in other markets and targeted special programs for movie production, minority communities, and government officials in the federal and state capitols.

Harry and I set out to build the wine writer community. At that time there were a few: Bob Misch, Bill Clifford, Philip Wagner and Creighton Churchill. Soon there were also Bob Balzer, Hank Rubin and Phil Hiaring working from Wine Institute. But Harry's salesmanship and my knowledge of newspapering (you could walk into newspapers then) combined to bring in a group which now reaches over 1,000. Of course this work is never done —the Academy of Wine Communications exists to help current wine writers and bring more into the field.

Those were halcyon days. Wine was getting better and more popular; the producers and the enthusiasts were an influential group; and then there was the Tasting of Paris and the *Time* cover story after all.

We learned that harvest news conferences worked well and treating wine like a business did not. I believe that between WI's PR budget and Robert Mondavi's commitment to PR I've spent around $25,000,000 over 38 years figuring out what does work.

In 1975, in one of the typical intra-industry squabbles, Italian Swiss Colony left Wine Institute, the agency was fired, Harry left and I was hired by WI as PR director. I inherited a lot of good programs left behind by Roy Taylor, Julius Jacobs, Larry Cahn and Marjorie Lumm. We launched some excellent programs: the PBS wine tasting series; Wine Media Day, which brought wineries and media together on a large scale for the first time; the Winery Guide to Public Relations; the Society of Wine Educators; the California Wine Program for U.S. Embassies and Consulates; and an outreach to the alcohol issues community.

But then the industry trade association's priorities were pruned to only one –politics –as Gallo and John De Luca decided to focus on government work alone. (Don't get me started on this subject.) So when Bob Mondavi married his PR director, Margrit Biever, Harry Serlis recommended me for that position.

In addition to quality wine and a marvelous winery site, public relations played a major role in building the winery. Bob had a vision and a commitment to tell his story as often and in as many places as he could. My job was to extend the reach and to help based on my experience. As Wine Institute shrank its role, we expanded ours.

In 1986 Bob launched his Mission program with the avowed purpose of defending wine against its anti-alcohol opponents. Among other aspects, we hosted a series of conferences featuring health researchers, sociologists, anthropologists and other scientists and artists who examined the basic soundness of wine in positive lifestyles for most people. One of our early speakers was Dr. Curtis Ellison of Boston University, who was thus brought into the wine community, enjoyed it, and through a chain of circumstances became the protagonist for the famous 60 Minutes pro-wine program that changed the role of wine in America.

Time moves on and programs wax and wane. The Robert Mondavi Winery went public, marketers often want the specificity of advertising buys, and it was time for me to move on as well. I went back 50 years to my own agency days, keeping Robert Mondavi as a client but specializing in reviewing and consulting on public relations programs for wineries and wine organizations. And so the story should have ended.

But one afternoon a close friend from the Mondavi days, Gary Ramona, called and asked me to come and talk to his boss, Fred Franzia, who was building a facility in Napa and had a number of brands. We began to work together successfully, so when Fred called and said he was bringing back the Charles Shaw brand for Trader Joe's, I just started a new file and waited for Fred or Gary or marketing consultant Brian Loomis to give me some details.

The details never came, but this latest chapter is in the book. So far Charles Shaw has had neither press release nor tasting program but the story has reached over 100,000,000 people and broken out of the wine columns and into general media. Writing its story for *Wines & Vines* gave me the idea for this book, and you know the rest.

I appreciate the collegiality of mostly all of us in wine PR, the support of my family, and the fun we've had along the way.

Harvey Posert

Napa Valley

A special acknowledgement goes to Greg Walter, editor and publisher of *Pinot Report,* for suggesting "Spinning the Bottle" as a title.

A View from a Wine PR Outsider:
Introduction by Paul Franson

In 1996 I moved to Napa Valley to pursue my long-time personal interest in wine by starting to write full time about wine and related subjects. Before that, I had written only sporadically about the subject, including a short stint as editor of the long-forgotten home-winemaking magazine, the *Purple Thumb*.

I had spent many years in writing and public relations, however. I edited two magazines, worked for two others and wrote a column on high-technology PR and marketing for eight years.

I also spent many years in public relations, both at corporations like Motorola and managing my own agency, which was the second largest in Silicon Valley at the height of its boom with more than 50 employees and clients like Hewlett-Packard and Hitachi. We had even dabbled in wine PR as a favor to investors in other clients, including helping get wide publicity when the Baron Eric de Rothschild of Chateau Lafite Rothschild invested in Chalone Wine Group.

As I began to contact wine companies as a serious writer, however, I was amazed at the lack of sophistication and drive most exhibited in publicizing their products. Most wineries considered pouring tastes of wine for visitors "PR" and thought that sending the new releases of their wines to the wine press sufficient for getting attention.

Many felt that the only things that really mattered were getting scores over 90 (now it's 95!) from uber-guru Robert Parker – and the influential *Wine Spectator,* and that there was no reason to try to reach beyond a core group of committed wine lovers.

Over time, I discovered that there were some true wine PR experts and they tried to do a good job – but sometimes their companies' owners and managers did their best to torpedo them. I saw some of the best PR people in the business fired and effective departments disbanded when new executives wanted to assert their own influence.

That's one reason we've collected these anecdotes and case studies. They show what is possible when competent people develop and implement good programs. They even include counterexamples all practitioners will appreciate, including a good effort thwarted by trivial competition thanks to Keith Love and some tales of personal errors by Jan Wells.

We invite you to read and study these chapters and feel free to borrow (or steal) the ideas. Good PR *can* make a difference. Only a tiny part of the US population drinks wine regularly, for example, and maybe someone inspired by these examples can use his or her PR skills to help make wine truly a part of the American lifestyle.

Paul Franson

Napa Valley

Editors' note on the second edition of *Spinning the Bottle*

These cases studies and essays were submitted by the authors and underwent minimal editing. The opinions and recommendations are theirs alone, and we take no responsibility for any of their comments.

Only a few chapters were repeated from the first edition of *Spinning the Bottle* (five out of 52); those are well worth repeating. Others were updated and edited, but most of the material is new.

You'll note some overlap and redundancies, but those thoughts repeated are likely to be important. Most sections include ways to contact them if you have any questions. The chapters are first grouped the authors subject and a logical sequence for the basics, then in order of author's last name.

Harvey Posert and Paul Franson

The Fundamentals of Wine Public Relations

Wine Corporate, Marketing and Communications Strategy

Paul Franson

Conscientious winery executives constantly re-evaluate their businesses, looking for ways to reduce costs, increase revenue and identify competitive advantages for future growth. Few, however, devote sufficient attention to one of a corporation's most strategic weapons: communications.

In classic marketing, communications is simply part of the promotional mix used to implement overall strategy. To the traditionalist, true marketing strategies are such techniques as brand extension, market segmentation and geographic expansion. Communications is simply a means to support such techniques.

In truth, however, many companies have succeeded by using communications as a strategic tool, a long-term, well-planned effort that gives them a fundamental advantage over their competition. This is *strategic communications*.

Examples are legend: Intel, Apple, Gallo, Kendall-Jackson, Trinchero, Bonny Doon. All of these companies make good products, but not necessarily better products than their competitors. What distinguishes them is their emphasis on communications. They clearly regard it to be as important as product development or production, and they devote the same executive attention to communications that they do to other fundamental corporate functions.

These companies and their executives' visibility as leaders and spokesmen are only part of the proof. Even more so is the attention these companies devote to crafting messages and the care with which they make announcements. Have you noticed that some wine industry figures, whether small winery owners or executives of larger companies are quoted more, and seem more authoritative?

The classic example of an effective leader was Robert Mondavi, who came to be regarded as the voice of the whole industry and had enormous impact.

No one has really risen to take his place as the spokesman for the wine business; the executives who are widely quoted include mischievous Fred Franzia of Bronco Wine Company with his "Two Buck Chuck," announcements that wines shouldn't cost more than $10, or challenges to the establishment.

Yet with control of more than 40,000 acres of California vineyards and modern and skilled winemaking staff, Franzia is an important figure who chooses not to act like an important spokesman. Likewise, Randall Grahm of Boony Doon gets a lot of attention that helps his business, but no one asks him to speak for the industry.

One possible heir to the mantle is an unlikely one, Ted Baseler of Ste. Michelle Wines Estates in Washington. Though seemingly a bit out of the mainstream, the winery has been a benevolent giant in its home territory, encouraging other wineries for the good of all as Robert Mondavi did.

But he also bought legendary Stag's Leap Wine Cellars in Napa Valley, the company that made the Cabernet Sauvignon that shocked the world by beating the best of Bordeaux at the famed wine tasting in 1976. Ste. Michelle also owns Villa Mount Eden Vineyards and Conn Creek in California, and acquired Erath Vineyards, one of Oregon's leading wineries. This makes Ste. Michelle the only winery with holdings in the three important west coast wine-producing states.

He also has successful partnerships with Tuscany's powerhouse Antinori family and Ernst Lösen in Germany. Baseler always takes the high road in contrast to Franzia, which makes him an industry leader.

Another excellent spokesperson for the industry has been Gina Gallo, a talented winemaker and third generation of the famed Gallo family. Other than her, the Gallos have been pretty quiet, though that's slowly changing, while other large wine companies like Constellation, The Wine Group and Trinchero have also avoided the limelight. Ironically, Gina Gallo's French husband, Jean-Charles Boisset, has become a passionate advocate of California wine and its little recognized history in his purchases of venebable Buen Vista, DeLoach and Raymond Vineayrds.

By contrast, the late Jess Jackson and his wife Barbara Banke sometimes sought strong presence, speaking out on important issues, but then seem to withdraw from attention.

What is communications?

Of course, *communications* is a broad term. It encompasses all the techniques used to influence customers, distributors, restaurants, stores and bars (and investors for the few public wine companies). This includes the traditional crafts of advertising, direct mail, collateral, packaging, newsletters, publicity, trade shows and seminars. More recently, important new channels have opened both to the industry and directly to consumers –social media like Facebook and Twitter, bloggers, web pages and wine clubs.

But communications also includes contact with distributors, restaurants and bars, sales forces and, most powerful of all, direct contact between proprietors, winemakers and executives and customers including distributors and other resellers.

These communications channels differ significantly in their strengths. Some can best communicate *specific* information such as information about wines and scores.

Other channels are capable of communicating *complex messages* of excellence and quality that give some wineries significant competitive advantages over firms that simply promise new wines with higher scores or lower prices.

These complex messages are more powerful than specific ones, yet are more difficult to communicate. One of the premier media for complex messages is owners and winemaker, hence the importance of involving them in programs with important customers, whether intermediary resellers or consumers.

This is also an expensive channel, and one best utilized prudently. One excellent way to leverage executives is to let them meet with and influence important critics, writers, bloggers, educators, sommeliers and corporate buyers.

Almost as strong communications tools as executives themselves are the implied third-party endorsements of critics and writers, many resulting from traditional public relations activities. These include actual endorsement of wines, favorable reviews and ratings, and articles, blogs, talks or columns.

The strength of third-party articles is that it carries the implication that some authority has judged a winery and its wines qualitatively and elected to write about it, which is exactly what happens.

Public relations techniques are especially powerful tools in helping companies position themselves favorably against their competitors. Various strategies are employed in this process, including educating the market directly and through the media, exploiting alliances, asserting quality leadership and differentiating your company and its wines from competitors.

But in addition to communicating these complex messages, companies also need to convey specific messages if they want to turn positive feelings and attitudes into sales. That's the strength of other communications tools such as advertising, direct mail, tech sheets, web pages, social media and even distributor sales reps. These media can provide the very specific details that turn prospects into customers.

Of course, the skilled practitioner can mold the tools to his desires. Though advertising isn't as much used for expensive wine as in most luxury products, clever advertising campaigns for high-volume wines have created strong positions for brands such as Yellow Tail, and can accomplish much besides providing details.

One often-overlooked communications channel is sales representatives and resellers. Though everyone agrees that they are important, few companies provide them with adequate tools to help turn the sales process into a repeatable and efficient operation. Most simply provide tech sheets on wines and samples.

Unfortunately, most companies regard the different elements of communications as distinct entities. Few recognize the need for treating the process as a whole, optimizing their overall communications effort to best utilize the strength of each technique.

Those companies that do recognize the value of strategic communications tend to use it well, however. They are usually more visible and better respected than their competitors, and their executives help their companies acquire human personalities, not cold and faceless images.

It's obvious that the vintner, winemaker or even most other executives can't devote full time to communications, but he or she should help set the overall goals and strategy, then participate in the programs his communications staff and advisors plan.

As a long-time writer covering diverse industries, I know the impact that press-savvy owners and executives have on the media.

And as an advisor to companies, I saw the difference between those companies where executives regard communications as a key part of their job and those where they leave it to others.

I'm always amazed at the executive who's too busy to help shape key messages or meet with the press when these activities can have more positive impact on the company than almost anything else he or she can do.

Strategic communications can make a big difference to any company, but it's a tool that requires executive commitment and involvement. It can't be left to junior staff members – or even staff or an agency, no matter how experienced. They can only provide guidance about the process and assist in the implementation.

Ultimately, the CEO or owner must also be the CCO – chief communications officer – if a company is to use this important tool to gain a significant advantage over its competition.

Now lets look at some specifics of the process, marketing 101 if you will.

The strategic communications process

The strategic communications process is a familiar one to any student of business and marketing. The first step is to conduct the research needed to determine the existing situation – how your company and its products are perceived by the people you want to reach (The "publics" in public relations.)

This includes research within and outside a company to gauge the competitive environment, market needs, and strengths and weaknesses of a company and its products.

In other words, "What do our prospects believe?"

The second part of the strategic communications process is to analyze the results of the research and develop desirable positioning and key messages.

In other words, "What do we want them to believe."

The third step is to develop specific communications tactics, including advertising, public relations, direct mail and other communications methods.

Then, of course, you have to implement these programs successfully.

Finally, evaluate the results and use this evaluation to improve the quality of the process.

The rest of this chapter is devoted to these five processes.

Introduction to strategy

The terms objective, strategy and tactics come from war, as do many of the other words and attitudes used to describe corporate operations. (This has been the subject for many observations about modern corporate conduct!)

To the military, an objective is the position it wants to occupy, or, by extension, the situation it wants to be true.

A strategy is the overall long-term action that will be taken, whereas a tactic is a specific action.

An example: Julius Caesar wanted to conquer Britain (his objective, certainly a measurable one). His strategy was divide and conquer. He formed alliances with certain Celtic tribes against the others, providing the leverage that allowed the tribes to fight themselves into weakness so he could assert authority. Some of the tactics involved were attacking opponents' strongholds, setting up his own forts, and burning the villages and food of "civilians" who supported the enemy, forcing them into dependence on the Romans.

In more contemporary corporate terms, an *objective* is the desired situation, ideally stated in measurable terms. It is expressed in a noun or verbal phrase (*establishment*, or *to achieve*, for example).

A *strategy* is a long term action designed to give a company a sustainable advantage over its competitors. A strategy is always expressed as a verb, such as *educate* the market or *create* a new product category.

Likewise, a *tactic* is a specific action, such as write a release or conduct a media tour. It's also expressed as a verb, such as *write* or *conduct*.

Corporations have – or should have – an overall corporate strategy supported by marketing, engineering and production strategies and tactics.

In many firms, corporate and marketing strategy is well defined by corporate and marketing executives and their staff, and communications strategy is a natural outgrowth of this process.

Many companies turn to outside agencies and consultants for assistance in developing corporate and marketing strategy as well as communications strategy. Many of these people have backgrounds traditionally associated with public relations, blurring the line between general marketing and public relations expertise, but others come from research or other viewpoints.

Marketing strategy must be based on corporate strategy, but corporate strategy can derive from many sources.

There are really only three basic viable strategies for success for any company:

- Innovate
- Be the lowest cost supplier
- Exploit a specific market niche (or niches)

How a company chooses an optimum overall strategy is beyond the scope of this book, but the process is often obvious upon reflection. If a company's biggest strength is the ability to produce wine at low cost like Bronco Wine Co., for example, that should probably be its overall corporate strategy.

If it has superb product innovation capabilities, or unusual insight into distribution, it should be to innovate. Trinchero, owner of Sutter Home, does this exceptionally well, and one byproduct is that it has become a high-volume, low-cost supplier as well.

And for many firms, particularly those with limited resources, the best route to success is to divide and conquer –a technique Julius Caesar used to subdue an island inhabited by millions of warlike inhabitants with only 20,000 troops. For a winery, this might mean focusing on a specific variety or type of wine, or a geographic region, or like Screaming Eagle, the market for people who must have the most expensive wines available to impress their friends.

As may be apparent, most wineries really don't have a well-thought-out corporate strategy. If a firm is really driven by the need for a founder to become well known, impress his friends or live an elegant lifestyle, for example, it's unlikely to always make the right business decisions.

Just picking one of the three basic corporate strategies isn't enough, of course. The company must carefully decide which markets to serve, or wines to make, or where to focus its development and marketing dollars. This is its marketing strategy. It always takes a careful examination of markets to make those decisions.

Among the nuances of corporate strategy, for example, are vertical integration (owning vineyards and wine production facilities) versus reselling wine made by others (negociants), growing by acquiring other wine companies or buying wine versus developing new varieties or brands in-house.

The Byzantine legal situation of the wine business offers innumerable opportunities for innovation in specific niches, from Internet sales to wine clubs to direct to trade –if allowed by law. There are endless variations, a consequence of the complexity of the markets and the ingenuity of participants in the companies involved.

Once the winery's basic strategy –which ironically is based on good market knowledge –is known, it can decide on its marketing strategy. And only when this is known, can it effectively plan overall communications strategy and tactics.

Innovation as a corporate strategy

A prime corporate strategy is innovation. Examples from the wine world are legion, including varietal wines to move upscale from generic names like burgundy and chablis once applied to wines in California.

Other examples were the first reserve bottlings, Sutter Home's white Zinfandel and its Menage à Trois, and Robert Mondavi's

Fumé Blanc, which he thought sound better than Sauvignon Blanc at the time.

Mondavi also envisioned Opus One as a joint venture with France's famous Lafite Rothschild.

Jess Jackson helped create a whole new type and market for wine with his slightly sweet Vintners Reserve Chardonnay, and Tony Terlato upended the US market for imports with Santa Margherita Pinot Grigio.

Chandon created a new high-end category of American sparkling wine when it built a winery in Napa Valley, though many other foreign and U.S. wineries jumped in to this market, too.

Screw capped wines, single-serving plastic bottles, cardboard boxes, kegs —all are ways wineries have developed new products to differentiate themselves.

Being the low-cost supplier as a corporate strategy

Being the low-cost supplier is a prime strategy, and many companies have thrived on it. Fred Franzia of Bronco Wine Co. , for example, controls more than 40,000 acres of vines and sophisticated production facilities. Many negociants scour the market for cheap bulk wines while others look for bargains overseas, often importing the wine in giant bladders.

The greatest appeal of being a low-cost supplier is that everyone is always looking for a bargain. The problem, of course, is that there always seems to be someone who can go lower.

Exploiting market niches as a corporate strategy

Many wineries – whether they know it or not – use market segmentation as their basic corporate strategy, though they may not be very good at it. It just happens rather than occurring by design.

Wineries have focused on regions, women, millennials, mothers, ethnic groups, sports fans, followers or entertainers, often a result of owners situations or tastes, for example.

Clos La Chance offers both a vegan wine as well as one aimed at young mothers. Small Howell at the Moon has targeted China and New York to the exclusion of other areas.

Many small wineries only sell direct to consumers, which is becoming easier as restrictive laws change.

Trinchero and J. Lohr make wine with the alcohol removed to serve a large market for people who can't or don't want to drink, including pregnant women.

Sutter Home, Gallo (Barefoot) and others have jumped into the hot market for sweetish Muscat wines, a market especially strong among urban African-Americans but also reaching others who don't like traditional dry wines.

What is marketing?

Whatever the corporate strategy chosen, a company must develop a marketing (as well as development, financial and production) strategy to support its aims. There are as many definitions of marketing as their are marketers. Here's my definition:

Marketing is understanding and satisfying customer needs and wants.

That implies that marketing has a major function even before a product is developed. One of the jobs of a marketing organization is to understand trends in the market and how they will impact future demand. Only in this way will marketing be able to help develop successful new products.

Of course, marketing has an equally important role after the product is developed, in preparing and presenting it to customers –both intermediaries at distributors, stores, restaurants and bars, and to consumers.

One of the best ways to ensure that both ends of marketing are well represented is to have separate groups responsible for each.

One would be customer-oriented, the other product-oriented. The first, sometimes called strategic marketing, watches industry trends and also communicates with customers, develops strategic alliances, and suggests opportunities.

Product marketing, by contrast, focuses on existing wines and channel marketing on getting products through complex sales and distribution channels.

Let's look first at how strategic marketing functions.

Elements of marketing strategies

According to classic marketing theory, there are only five basic elements of marketing strategy (sometimes called the five *p*'s):

- Product
- Position
- Pricing
- Place (Distribution)
- Promotion (Communications)

Let's look briefly at each of the five elements of market to see how they relate to the operation of a typical wine company.

The product

There's little question that the right product plays a key role in any marketing strategy. But what is the right product?

Products can vary in many ways. Some of the characteristics that can affect product acceptance are taste, packaging and quality. Less obvious are such product differentiation as exclusivity versus broad appeal, and appeal to wine snobs and wine geeks.

In the ideal company. marketing has a great deal to do with product development. Although some companies have succeeded by developing innovative products that subsequently found a wide market, that's a chancy approach. For most companies, it's better to investigate market requirements and desires before developing a product. That's the function of industry marketing.

It's beyond the scope of this book to address product development. Instead, we will focus on the communications aspects of success.

Product position, on the other hand, is a critical element of communications as well as marketing. A position is the qualitative ranking of a product in the minds of customers. Another word for position is differentiation. Communicating a distinct position can be very important, and in fact, choosing and communicating a position is key to all successful marketing and public relations.

The price

Price is also a vital element in marketing. Products can be priced in many ways, and for many different reasons. The usual factors are cost of production (or acquisition), the perceived value of the product to the user, cost of comparable products, or even business philosophy. (If it's more expensive, many people think it must be better.) Aims of pricing strategy may be penetration of a market on one hand, or skimming its cream on the other.

An obvious way to price a wine is a percentage above the cost, which should allow adequate margins. This could be acceptable – even vital – in mature markets, but almost always restricts return on innovative products.

Pricing by value is the optimal way to price any product if possible. It's difficult to justify paying $150 or $250 for a bottle of wine in economic terms, but it works for some wines.

Conversely, some people always seek bargains. They bought Charles Shaw (Two Buck Chuck) because it was cheap, but kept buying it because they thought it was a good value.

The place

The place a customer can buy a product is very important in the success of most products. Products reach their buyers through many routes. The most familiar is the local wine store, supermarket (in many places) or restaurant, but there are many alternatives — including the way the product reaches that store.

Wine distribution is very complex. Many products are now sold through retail stores that buy from distributors. Direct to consumer techniques like the Internet and wine clubs become popular. Mass chains have had a huge impact. Laws in various states differ widely, too, so wine may or may not be sold in various channels.

Promotion

The last element in marketing success is promotion, notably communications. The most obvious way to communicate with prospects to most people is advertising. Vital in many markets is merchandising and promotion such as point of purchase displays, packaging and direct mail.

And, of course, another effective type of promotion is public relations, the focus of the rest of this book.

***

Paul Franson is a free-lance writer based in Napa Valley who specializes in wine, food, travel and wine country lifestyle. He was formerly a corporate and agency public relations specialist, working at Motorola and Teradyne and founding Franson & Associates, Inc., which reached 55 employees and assisted high-tech clients in Silicon Valley such as Hewlett-Packard, Hitachi and LSI Logic.

He also was a writer/field editor for two technical magazines and edited a hobby magazine and a high-tech business magazine. He has published three books on marketing and public relations.

New Perspectives on Marketing Research
Marc Engel

Conducting marketing research in the wine industry is like hugging a porcupine. It's hard to wrap your arms around, and you better know what you're doing or else you'll get hurt.

The challenge is endemic to wine itself. With what other product do consumers get so overwhelmed by something so pleasurable, where …

- They doubt their own taste buds and defer to the opinions of "experts" to tell them what they should and shouldn't like –and are made to feel inferior for liking what they like (e.g., something sweet)?
- They struggle to describe the smells and tastes they're experiencing?
- They may be uncertain of whether it's the grape, blend, region or producer that they like, or even which is which when they look at the label?
- They may underestimate the role of the food, the people and the setting in which they enjoyed the wine?
- They face a "Tower of Babble" (yes, homonym intended) at the retail wine shelf? Is it any wonder many struggle to remember brand names, or are "pretty certain" they've heard of brands with Mad Libs-generated names like Yak Creek, Grouse Meadow or Gerbil Ridge?
- These factors make it difficult to find the right consumers, ask them direct questions and receive reliable answers. But if you wanted things to be easy, you wouldn't be in the wine business, would you?

That said, marketing research, even in the wine industry, is not brain surgery. It takes common sense, an ability to walk in other people's shoes, and some elbow grease. It is as much art as it is science. It is not intended to dictate what to do, but rather to inform your decision-making. You should know your industry well enough to put consumer research in context, not rely on it blindly.

Marketing research can also be a brand-building tool, closely linked to public relations. (That's why I'm being paid the big bucks to write this chapter.) [Ha! says PF]

A quick review

Marketing is about attracting consumers' attention, converting them to buyers of your brand, retaining them as customers, and growing the relationship with them so that they become your advocates. The research you conduct should always serve one or more of these purposes.

Research is about gaining perspective. You should seek input from current customers, prospective customers, lapsed customers, key players in the trade and your employees, so you have a full picture of what your products and brands mean to various constituencies. You should also explore the context for their interaction –how your brands fit within their wine worlds as well as within their worlds generally. Without all these perspectives, you risk diminishing your brand and losing business.

Big picture perspective

To put your products and brands in context, it helps to have the framework of market trends.

Nielsen and Symphony IRI track how well products and brands are selling vis-à-vis the competition, and how well different varietals, wine-producing regions and price points are selling. Wine Market Council's annual survey of wine drinkers measures self-reported behaviors and attitudes related to wine and other aspects of their lifestyle. Industry-wide segmentations, such as Constellation's "Project Genome" and UK-based Wine Intelligence's "Portraits", cluster wine consumers by differentiating attitudes and behavior, and offer estimates of their relative on- and off-premise value.

This information is useful –and not merely cocktail chatter –to the extent that you draw insights that pertain to your business. But general industry research is only part of the picture.

A custom perspective

Ultimately, you need to understand what your current customers want and need so you can nurture your relationship with them, and what your prospective customers want and need so you can draw them into your brand. You need research about your wine, your brand and your customers.

You don't need to hire a professional researcher for everything (though my contact info does appear at the end of the chapter). You do need to be open to the myriad opportunities to gain perspective, some of which are already at your fingertips.

Mine your own business

You are sitting on a wealth of information about people who have (or had) an affinity for your brand. Start with your wine club, arguably the customers closest to your brand. If you don't already know who your most valuable customers are, figure it out. Assess their buying patterns and interactions with you and identify patterns you can use to your advantage –by your advantage, I mean their advantage: to serve their wants and needs better to deepen their connection with you. Do the same thing with lagging or even lapsed club members.

Engage in a conversation

Many of you are probably mining your club data already. But how are you applying what you learn? Have you shown gratitude to your most valuable customers? Are you reaching out to customers who may have drifted, to help bring them back? Ask them why they've drifted, what else they've been buying. Do so in a non-confrontational way that shows humility and doesn't take them for granted. Offer incentives to return.

Empower them as teachers who can educate you about your brand. Invite them to share their stories and opinions about:

- The foods and occasions on which they enjoy your wines
- What they like most about your wine and your story
- What other wines they drink (it's okay to acknowledge that they're not monogamous)
- What they feel distinguishes your brand from the competition
- Suggestions for improvements

You don't need to follow every suggestion they make, but maybe you learn something about your brand you can use in communications, tasting notes or conversations with the trade. Even if you don't, the very act of asking customers for their opinions deepens the connection they feel with your brand. They feel their opinion matters and that you care about them, which is a reason to turn to you rather than other brands that don't care.

The more you know about your customers, the better able you are to serve them. In addition to asking about your wines, find out more about your customers personally. For example, ask what other activities and interests they have, whether related to wine directly, indirectly (e.g., food, travel) or not at all. This information presents opportunities for personalized shows of appreciation, perhaps on their birthdays or a random day, just because you care.

As wine and business guru Gary Vaynerchuk, whom you ignore at your peril, notes in *The Thank You Economy*:

"[C]ustomers' demands for authenticity, originality, creativity, honesty and good intent have made it necessary for companies and brands to revert to a level of customer service rarely seen since our great-grandparents' day, when business owners often knew their customers personally, and gave them individual attention."

Social Media

Technology, in particular social media, has empowered consumers to be heard and influence brands like never before. It has also enabled myriad easy, inexpensive ways for brands to build engaging relationships with them.

Even if you don't have a wine club, or even a winery, you can easily connect with —and ask similar questions of —the people who are buying your wine at stores, bars and restaurants, or elsewhere online.

You do have a Facebook fan page, right? Learn about your Facebook fans the way you learn about your wine club members. The connections you make with customers through social media has a gigantic multiplier effect. Think about how quickly people can and brag —or conversely, gripe —about you to their friends. And Facebook is just one of many tools.

In addition to what you learn from the consumers who have taken the time to connect with the brand, you can also learn from those who are talking about you, but not to your face(book). It's much easier than it used to be for consumers to do their research, with the explosion of wine-related sites, blogs, YouTube, Twitter, smartphone apps and who knows what else by the time this book is printed (and Kindled, Nooked, iPadded...).

Not only can you hear what's being said, you can participate in the conversation. When the talk is positive, reach out and show appreciation. When it's negative, understand the concerns and address them. Companies like Cruvee quantify online chatter, but even if one or two people express a concern, others may be experiencing similar feelings. You need to be aware of potential problems and get out in front of them –it's like pre-emptive crisis management.

You need to research what's being said not only about your brands, but also about your competition for additional context to help you differentiate your offerings.

Inside perspective

Another perspective is that of your employees, especially the ones closest to your customers: sales, customer service, tasting room and club. These employees stand at the intersection of the brand and your customers, absorbing a constant stream of valuable information. Empower them to reply directly to concerns when possible or at least take ownership to find out answers. Solicit their feedback on how to improve the business, whether about products, pricing, placement or communications.

Trade perspective

You should seek the input of distributors, retailers, wine buyers, F&B directors and sommeliers when you are developing new concepts, packages, communications, etc. They have a unique perspective on your brand compared to everything else they sell. They remain vital gatekeepers, as many consumers still seek guidance. Just as connecting with consumers builds a connection with your brand, so, too, does reaching out to the trade. In addition to conducting research, you are encouraging them beyond just the immediate dollars to care more about your brand. (Talk about hugging a porcupine!)

A professional research perspective

In addition to the research you should be conducting on your own, you should periodically want the counsel of a professional researcher. Engaging a trained researcher adds the objectivity and gravitas that may be needed to convince investors, distributors and retailers of consumer interest in a new concept you're developing: products, packaging, communications, promotions, etc. Such engagement can help increase mindshare and market share and, ultimately, the bottom line.

Professional researchers know how to design strategies to meet your research objectives and marketing goals, design unbiased surveys, improvise during an interview or group discussion, interpret nonverbal communications, discern differences between what people say and what they mean, evaluate multiple data points and derive insights.

Clients default to focus groups, but there are many options for qualitative input. With something as personal as wine, focus groups – at least as they've traditionally been run – could actually lead you down the wrong path. In-home parties are a fun, productive group alternative. Removed from the fluorescent lights and one-way mirrors associated with focus group facilities (and cop shows), a qualified consumer receives a catered dinner and invites qualified friends for an informal discussion over great food and wine.

One-on-one interchanges are useful for many projects. With package testing, for example, you need to talk with individuals since their reactions are so subjective. Since they're made in an instant, all you need are quick impressions –the more time one spends looking a bottle in a contrived research setting, the further away it is from how consumers would actually shop in a store.

Purchasing wine at a store is contextual –consumers notice items that stand out from what's around it. Thus, you may want to conduct shop-alongs or in-store observations and on-the-spot interviews (called, "intercepts") for a better sense of how consumers respond when they face thousands of choices.

Ethnographies, personal blogs and short films offer opportunities to go more in-depth about individual consumers in their "natural habitat." Rather than the typical question-answer approach, the subject tells her or his story, and you distill the lessons for your brand later. These techniques are particularly useful as context for concept development, and you don't need that many to form a useful picture.

Just as wine marketers need to reach wine consumers where they are —geographically and psychologically —so do wine marketing researchers. Enabling easy feedback through mobile devices, such as through tailored apps, will be one way to reach your customers when they're in stores and at restaurants and bars.

Creative perspectives

Sometimes you need to go out of focus to get into focus. That's why I developed Out-of-Focus Groups. It's an approach that integrates research and ideation, and often reaches outside the primary business —sometimes to the arts —for a unique perspective.

I recently conducted an Out-of-Focus Group for a wine client that needed marketing program ideas. We brought together key players within the brand, including the CEO and global marketing director, and combined them with "friends" of the brand, including a distributor, a writer, and a food and style editor.

I partnered with a fellow improvisational comedian and incorporated improv into the session. The creativity that emerges when people are willing to let their guards down and get out of their heads is remarkable. Improv levels the playing field, unleashing a sea of ideas from everyone, which participants then developed in breakout sessions. At the end of the day we evaluated the ideas and settled on one that was put into practice. Not only was the session rewarding, everyone had nearly illegal levels of fun!

A cultural perspective

None of us lives in a vacuum (though many live in cocoons). The culture around us shapes our viewpoints. Thus it's important to stay attuned to cultural shifts that affect the way people behave as their wine-consumer selves. That's why I partner with an applied cultural analyst, expert at deciphering the signs and codes that underpin our perceptions and interactions with the world around us.

A final perspective

No single source of information alone —whether you uncover it on your own or learn from a professional researcher —is sufficient. By walking in the shoes of different constituencies, you gain multiple perspectives that help you form a picture of how your products and brands are perceived, so that you can make better marketing decisions to attract, retain and empower your customers. You might even learn how to hug that porcupine.

***

Marc Engel is the founder of Engel Research Partners (www.engelrp.com), a company that integrates research and creativity to help clients across multiple categories gain perspective on their brands, products, packaging, external and internal communications. A former partner with B/R/S Group, Marc spearheaded its pioneering research on the Two Buck Chuck phenomenon and conducted proprietary research for wine clients worldwide. Marc has been a panelist and moderator at wine events in the U.S. and abroad. His unique perspective is shaped largely by writing and performing comedy. Reach Marc at marc@engelrp.com.

Some Tips on Wine Public Relations
Paul Franson

I spent 20 years in corporate and agency public relations. I worked for four magazines 13 years, editing two, and have written about wine as a freelancer for more than 15 years. With that experience in mind, here are my tips on public relations for wineries.

- Decide what's distinctive about your winery and its wines. Don't try to be all things to all people unless you're very large (and probably not even then).

- Make a list of the 10 or 12 writers most important to your winery, and try to get to know them in person. That may not be possible with top writers, who may not be available or interested. Invite others over for a meeting, tour if relevant and tasting –and the relationship is best cemented with lunch. And though writers appreciate and often become friends with PR people, they're really interested in talking to the owner, chief executive or winemaker.

- There's no such thing as a typical "wine writer." People who write about wine have many different interest and priorities. Determine each writer's interest: it may only be tasting and rating wine, but it could be much wider. Writers who cover wine range from part-timers doing it for perks to serious journalists who treat the job just like covering politics or business. Be honest but careful with the latter.

- Develop a list of people who write about wine, but don't overuse it.

- Make sure your web site includes contact information and your marketing information. A great bonus is thumbnails of photos available online or otherwise; many writers don't have budgets for pictures.

- Many writers don't regularly rate wines, but sending samples helps them know what you're doing. Ask before sending wine samples, however. Not all writers want them, some don't or can't accept them, and some prefer to ask for specific samples.

- What's news? Something truly new. A new wine release is not normally news. A new type of wine from your winery may be. Most writers don't consider awards a big deal.

- It doesn't hurt to send club newsletters and notices of events to writers (but ask first). Telling writers about events isn't an invitation. If you want writers to attend, invite them but remember that there are dozens held monthly here.
- Don't expect writers to provide market research, i.e., honest opinions on your wine. Some writers love to give you their views, but they supposedly work for their readers, not you.
- Respond quickly. Wine media may be laid back compared to most publications, but they still have deadlines. Include your cell number if that's the best way to reach you.

Use the web to reach the media as well as customers

The Internet allows wineries to bypass editorial "gatekeepers" who they think first ignore them, then distort what they've said. Now those wineries can say what they want directly to viewers who visit their Web pages. The same is true for Twitter and Facebook.

That makes these types of communications very important for most wineries. Be sure to have a website with information about your business. For most wineries, it's mostly a marketing tool as much or more than a sales channel.

Likewise, Tweeting news of events and specials, as well as developing and using Facebook, are almost vital in today's environment. But don't forget other channels, too. The immediacy of these forms of communication often make users forget that important media require more time to publish material and many people don't use Facebook or Twitter but do read magazines, newspapers and newsletters, listen to the radio and watch television.

In the rush to use the Internet to bypass the press, however, many wineries miss an opportunity: to make it easy for writers to get the right information in the first place. That's primarily email and Web pages, not Twitter and Facebook.

I've found the Internet, especially the Web pages of wineries, can be an immense timesaver. But not always.

Many wineries overlook basics that could tell their story better and get favorable press coverage. They should remember that their Web sites are really advertising and promotional material. They should receive as much consideration as ads.

Here are some suggestions to improve web sites. Most help prospects visiting your Web site just as much as writers.

- Be on the Web even if it's only a simple page containing your contact information. But a good site should be a high priority.
- List your address, direct phone, cell phone and your e-mail – and check and answer your email.
- List your current releases and specials on line. If they change frequently, note that they are just typical. List prices, too.
- Post biographies and photos of your winemaker, owner and other key people, your exterior and interiors and vineyards on your web site, preferably as small thumbnails leading to high-resolution photos writers can download.
- Keep the site current and post all your news releases to the web site.
- Don't go crazy with graphics, much less video, audio and multimedia. People who seek your web site are looking for information, not entertainment.
- Be on the Web, preferably with your own domain, even if it's only a page containing your phone number and a notice, "This site is under construction." But don't leave it that way for very long; posting a superb site should be a high priority.
- List the address, phone and if possible, the general e-mail of your headquarters. Even if your firm has locations all over the world, writers and customers need to start somewhere.
- Designate someone to receive, acknowledge and route inquiries from any source, not be a busy technician but someone sensitive to customer needs.
- List media contacts with a name, phone and e-mail. The public, not just the press, may contact them, but they can forward inquires to the right source. Include cell numbers if that's the best way to reach the contact.
- Provide background with detailed information on your winery, its products, its operations and its history.
- Post executive biographies, titles, downloadable photos (but not big photos on the page), and their e-mail addresses and

phone numbers. Someone can screen the inquiries, but I suspect executives would find inquiries interesting.

- Provide financial reports on line if your firm is public, preferably in ordinary text, Word or Web formats.
- Keep the site current, including releases and prices.

Some hints for writing press releases

A news release is simply a document that tells a writer, reporter or commentator about something that's happened – or will happen. It's not an article or "story." Leave that to the recipient writer.

If you'd like your material used, make using it as easy as possible. There are a number of conventions that make it easy for busy writers to use the material.

- Provide the facts, the five "W's": who, what, why, where, when – and you might include a sixth—who cares? Most writers need prices, too. A news release isn't an article, a letter to customers or distributors, an ad, an e-mail promotion or a brochure. Don't write an article; leave that to the writer.
- Write a simple headline that gives a summary; don't try to be cute, especially if it hides the news. You can provide a subhead if you want to expand on a few important points.
- State the significance of the release in the first sentence. Don't sneak up to it in the third paragraph, and don't brag.
- Stick to the facts. Forget the flowery phrases and especially all the superlatives. In general, avoid first ("we, our" and second ("you") person.
- If you include quotations from your executives or staff, make them punchy and meaningful. Most quotes in releases are unusable drivel: "We're happy to announce that we've hired my talented daughter as CEO…"
- It's best to provide all the basic information in one page. You can include more information if you want, but a release rarely justifies more than a couple of pages. It's better to provide background material in other documents.
- Provide a link to high-resolution photographs and other art on your website so that writers can download them if they want. Thumbnails are useful, too. Don't e-mail large attachments. Let people request them if they want.

- You can single-space the text; in the old days double-spacing was desirable for editing, but now most editors edit on screen or print out copy double-spaced.
- Send as simple text or Word, not pdfs and never as images (including pdf images!) Designers like pdfs because readers can't change the look, but writers need to cut, pastes, edit and adapt.
- Provide a contact who will be available for clarification, amplification or other information. Include name, phone number and e-mail address.

Some common style errors and suggestions

These are rules from the Associated Press Style Book, used by virtually all newspapers and most magazines and other publications.
- Don't assume the reader will know industry terms, abbreviations and jargon.
- Forget the "pleases" (e.g., "Please call 777-1200." Just say "Call 777-1200," or "The telephone number is 777-1200.")
- Use a.m., p.m., not PM or pm.
- Write out most symbols (use "and" for "&," "percent" for "%" but not "$.")
- Don't abbreviate most words. This includes days of the week.
- Abbreviate "St." "Ave." and "Blvd." when in addresses with numerals (but not if they're used without numbers, e.g., "The market is on Main Street").
- Write dates as Sept. 11, 2006. Don't include "th," etc., and abbreviate longer months (Don't abbreviate April, May, June or July). And
- Don't use extra zeros with money($5, not $5.00) or times (10 p.m., not 10:00 p.m.), but obviously write 10:30 p.m.
- Use conventional state abbreviations ("Wash., Calif.," not two-letter postal codes after cities in text. Write out the name if you're referring to the whole state: "Washington wine."
- Write telephone numbers as (707) 258-0159 (not 258.0159). The AP prefers 1-707-258-0159.

Formatting and distribution of news releases
- Don't use ALL CAPITALs, or Capitalize The First Letters Of All Words, or underline text or use bold. Use normal

fonts and forget color. I recommend Times Roman or similar serif font, and avoid "arty" fonts and italics. Write in sentences and punctuate normally.

- Use e-mail or maybe a paid service for releases unless told otherwise. Place information in text of message or use Word documents. Don't send releases as large attachments or Acrobat (.pdf) files.
- Most writers don't want fax or paper: they have to retype anything that comes as fax or printed releases or try to scan it, which is time-consuming and can introduce errors.
- Be sure to include a subject and note in the email with an attached release. Many people won't open unknown attachments (and for good reason).
- Make it easy for a writer to cut and paste, which encourages him to use it. It also minimizes mistakes. Don't use locked Adobe Acrobat files (pdfs), Microsoft Publisher files or other unusual formats for releases if you want anyone to publish them, and don't *ever* send a photograph of the text (a jpg).
- It's great to send FaceBook, evite and Twitter reminders of events, but if you want publications and websites to use them, send text or Word in emails.
- Make releases and artwork available on your web site the day you post it.
- Be familiar with deadlines. Don't send announcements late..

An Example of a Basic News Release

Contact: Paul Franson
(707) 258-0159
paul@napalife.com

Napa Valley Winery Opens Tasting Room

NAPA VALLEY, Calif., April. 18, 2015 – Wappo Winery in Calistoga in Napa Valley has opened a tasting room open to visitors with appointments daily.

The tasting room is the winery's first. It showcases the winery's Sauvignon Blanc, Cabernet Sauvignon and Zinfandel wines, which are available for tasting and purchase.

The tasting room is open daily except major holidays from 10 a.m. to 4 p.m. A flight of five tastes is $20.

Call (707) 555-1212 to make appointments. The winery is at 5555 Silverado Trail in Calistoga. Its web site is www.wappo.com.

–end –

Tips for Dealing with the News Media
Kimberly Flowers

Free media exposure is one of the best tools you have to communicate with consumers, increase brand awareness and help position your winery and your brands with multiple audiences.

Following are a few simple tips to keep in mind when communicating with the news media.

Always remember:

- When dealing with the press, you are always on the record. Imagine that everything you say could end up on the front page of the paper.
- When speaking to the press, you are representing your winery and/or family. What you say should be consistent with the mission and goals of your organization.
- Members of the press are just trying to do their job, and so are we. Treat them fairly and they will (we hope) give an objective assessment of the issue, product or announcement.

Do's

- Respond within 24 hours. Many opportunities can disappear if you are not responsive. On the other hand, if a story is potentially damaging, not responding will leave the reporter to his own devices to get the story. Ask the reporter his deadline and then be responsive.
- Be prepared. Before the interview, think of potential questions the reporter might ask. Then practice saying your key message points to get comfortable with your answers.
- Familiarize yourself with the reporter. If you have time before the interview, familiarize yourself with the reporter and the publication. Do an Internet search to get a sense of what he writes on and how he reports.
- Be courteous and friendly. Even if a reporter is confrontational, be friendly and don't lose your cool.
- Know your topic. Brush up on the specifics of the topic you are going to discuss before the interview.

- Be honest. Tell the truth. Never, never lie. If you don't know the answer to a question, say so.
- Be concise. Get to your point immediately. Long, rambling answers tend to blur the key messages you are trying to convey.
- Stay on message. If you prepare before the interview, know two or three key talking points that best represent what you are trying to accomplish and incorporate those into the discussion. Repeat them often.
- Be quotable. Try to say something during the interview that is memorable and can be quoted.
- Use anecdotes/facts. The most effective communicators are storytellers. Use anecdotes and facts to emphasize your points.
- Offer additional sources. Depending on the focus of the story, have in mind additional sources the reporter can use.
- Use the questions as an opportunity. Every question is an opportunity to promote your winery and reinforce your key message points.

Don'ts

- Never say "No comment." You will look as though you have something to hide. Instead say, "I can't provide, or release, that information at this time." Briefly explain why. Again, if you don't know the answer, say so.
- Don't use jargon or buzzwords. Don't assume the audience or the reporter knows wine industry terminology. Try to convey your ideas using language everyone can grasp.
- Don't go off the record. If you don't want to see or hear what you say, don't say it.
- Don't let reporters put words in your mouth. If a reporter says, "What you're saying is…" and it's not accurate, correct the misstatement immediately, and then restate your position.
- Don't guess, speculate or answer hypothetical. questions. If something isn't certain, you don't have all the facts, don't guess. If the reporter asks a "What if" question, don't speculate. You have no idea how a story will turn out if you speculate.

- Don't feel compelled to answer a loaded question directly. If you are asked a question that clearly sets you up for disaster, don't answer it directly. Bridge your response back to one of your key messages that underscore the positive.
- Don't respond to a question about another winery or vintner. Speak for yourself and what you know best. If a reporter wants to know what other wineries think or do, suggest he call them directly.
- Don't ask to see the article before it's published. This is taboo. Good reporters will never offer up their work before it's finished.

Answering hostile/difficult questions

- If you feel a question is unfair, let the reporter know.
- If a reporter repeats a question or tries to ask it in different ways, repeat your answer (he is simply trying to get you to say something different).
- If there is extended silence on the line, don't feel obligated to fill it. It's a tactic to get you to keep talking. Once you've made your point, stop talking.

After the interview

- Always provide promised follow-up materials in a prompt manner.
- If the reporter did a good job and you like the story, call or e-mail him with a word of thanks. But remember that he is working for his medium, not to make friends.
- If you feel you were misquoted or misrepresented, evaluate the significance of the error. If it is small, let it go. If it's a problem, contact the reporter to set the record straight. If it's a disaster and the reporter completely misrepresented you, consider a letter to the editor or other measures. Understand, this last option will likely alter your future relationship with the reporter.
- If you are contacted about a story by a major print or broadcast outlet (e.g., *New York Times*, *Washington Post*, *Today Show*, etc.) notify the communications director at your trade association, who may be able to provide assistance and/or guidance in maximizing the opportunity.
-

***

Kimberly L. (Getto) Flowers has spent more than twenty years in the world of public affairs and public relations, beginning her career in Washington, D.C., working for two Members of Congress, and later, as a presidential appointee, to the Department of State and the U.S. Small Business Administration during the Reagan Administration.

In 1991, Flowers relocated to Moscow, Russia to open an office for the San Francisco-based public relations firm, The PBN Company. She managed public relations programs in the former Soviet Union for public and private sector clients such as Chevron, Pepsi-Cola International, Conoco, the World Bank and U.S. AID. From 1993 to 1997, Flowers managed privatization public awareness programs in Moldova, Armenia, Russia and Uzbekistan. From 1997 to 2000, she worked as a director in the San Francisco office of Burson-Marsteller for Sun Microsystems, Golden State Warriors, Andersen Consulting and Philip Morris, among others.

Using Celebrities to Sell Products and Services

Rene A. Henry

For years advertisers have been paying top dollar to get entertainers and athletes to endorse and sell their products. Companies associate their products or services with a celebrity hoping that will transfer to a potential buyer and ultimately the bottom line.

There are both direct and indirect ways to get a product endorsement. One is to pay the celebrity for services that include broadcast commercials, print advertisements and personal appearances. Another is to get a product displayed and used in a feature motion picture or television series or special or at a televised or filmed event.

Recognizing the love that entertainers have for athletes and vice-versa, in the 1960s the Wine Institute introduced a public relations tool to give prestige to California wines by having a celebrity host a tasting of California wines for friends and colleagues. Each event provided a series of photo opportunities, television clips, feature stories and column items in daily newspapers, magazines and the entertainment trades.

Actor Vincent Price was retained as a celebrity spokesperson. Daniel J. Edelman, the public relations firm for Wine Institute, placed Price on various television network talk shows, including The Tonight Show with Johnny Carson. Price also hosted a wine tasting at his home every year for his friends – some of the biggest names in Hollywood – and selected media.

If anyone doubts the love affairs between entertainers and athletes, all one needs to do is watch a Lakers basketball game in Los Angeles with Jack Nicholson and other superstars at courtside. Celebrities turn out when the Knicks play in Madison Square Garden and television cameras are on them at tennis, football and other sports events.

The Edelman agency also sought out celebrities known to have an interest in wine. They were selected to host wine tastings at their homes. Successful, celebrity-loaded wine tastings included ones hosted by Glenn Ford, a graduate of Paris' Le Cordon Bleu, and Jerry Perenchio to honor Andy Williams.

All costs for the events, including wine, food and entertainment, were paid for by the Wine Institute. This became a great way not only to showcase California wines but to introduce many previously French-wine-only drinkers to a wine comparable in taste and quality and significant in value and at less cost.

Whenever a spokesperson is retained it is important to have clauses in any agreement regarding morality and ethics and other issues that could impact the product. All specifics regarding the endorsement, personal appearances and what can and cannot be said must be very carefully spelled out. It is important to stipulate that the sponsor's representatives have direct access to the celebrity and not be at the "mercy" of either the agent or the publicist. The latters' interests are only those of their client and few have an understanding of the "big picture" and overall public relations strategy.

This also is true when approached by a representative of a celebrity who wants free wine, champagne, cheese and accoutrements to host an event. There must be direct access by a representative of the company and the celebrity involved.

Sometimes wine writers or entertainment columnists worked with the Edelman agency to host their own wine tasting. Most were always accommodated. Sometimes the tasting would be limited to comparing selected varietal California and French wines in a blind tasting. All of the events became strong endorsements for California wines.

California wines and champagne also were made available to the mayor's office in Los Angeles for various special events as well as at charitable functions attended by celebrities.

California wines also were written into scripts of motion pictures and television programs as well as used as props. This meant contacting writers, directors and producers as well as the property masters at the various studios throughout Hollywood. It was important to always establish standards and have an agreement with those responsible for production of the program so in no way was California wine ever depicted in a negative way. Certainly no one would have wanted a mention of California wines in *Days of Wine and Roses!*

When you watch a television program or see a motion picture with a particular automobile or very visible product, this didn't just happen. Public relations firms with special entertainment divisions and specialty placement firms are retained by companies to get their products placed in front of cameras.

The most advantageous placement of a product is in a feature motion picture because of its longevity. First it will be shown in first run theaters, then in second run theaters before being on a pay-for-view cable network. Then the program becomes available on VHS or DVD for home viewing and then on any number of cable television channels. All one has to do is look at a TV guide and see the number of old movies and programs being rerun. Some films can have a life of 20 or more years, making the initial investment to get the product displayed a bargain.

***

Rene A. Henry lives in Seattle, Washington, and is the author of seven books. He writes on a variety of subjects including sports, crisis management and communications, customer service, travel and tourism, and higher education. Many of his widely published articles are posted on his website at www.renehenry.com. His latest book, Communicating In A Crisis, is a must read for anyone in senior management. He is a member of the Academy of Motion Picture Arts & Sciences and the Academy of Television Arts & Sciences and spent five decades of his career in sports public relations.

Wine Events: Great PR or a Big Waste of Cash?

Sara Cummings

We have all heard it at one time or another: Let's do a huge event to draw attention to our brand/winery! Let's get "the media" to come! (Please note that "the media" is used in a tone that creates the impression that they are a herd of cattle grazing together in some nearby meadow as they await your invitation and phone call. Accordingly, "the media" is expected to respond *en masse* to any wine-related invitation that arrives, attend the event and love it, and then write a glowing article.)

If you have ever proceeded with a large wine event, you know what comes next. A budget that grows beyond all reason, an event dominated by style rather than substance, and a huge drain on your time (and usually the time of the entire *ad hoc* committee who get sucked into the project), and then many expectant gazes from management assuming that the minute the event ends there will be countless feature articles about the event and the winery.

In my thirteen years in wine PR, I have seen some events truly pay off in terms of delivering key marketing messages, generating media ink and positive coverage, but I have also witnessed many events that were not so successful. In the challenging marketplace we are all navigating, some of these excessive expenditures have become historic mementos of the "go-go" late 1990s. But it seems like more wine events continue to take place every week, especially in key wine markets.

Now, more than ever, it is important for wine PR people to ask the tough questions at the beginning of the event, shape the event to achieve the winery's goals, and manage expectations along the way – or decide that there are better ways to achieve the desired goal.

What makes a winery pr event successful?

I joined a company some years ago in the midst of a huge PR event plan created by their outside agency. The events involved "shipping in" the most distinctive elements of the winery to New York and Miami to a venue where trade and media guests were invited for the evening.

On my first day of work, I was flown to the Miami event, which cost over $60,000 (in the late 1990s) before the agency retainer and many other expenses were factored into the equation. The attendance was lighter than anticipated, with many last-minute cancellations. Everyone who attended enjoyed the event, and perhaps left the event knowing more about the winery than when they arrived there, but that was the whole outcome. No feature articles, no splashy coverage, and as far as I know, the reputation of the wines remained the same.

The sister event held two weeks before in New York was a great lesson in the "luck" factor of getting good event attendance. The Yankees were suddenly in the play-offs, and many New Yorkers who had planned to attend now had a new, more important engagement. Over $100,000 was invested in the New York event, and it would be hard to justify with results, from trade or media.

So, enough about how *not* to do a successful event. I believe that a successful PR event (wine or otherwise) includes the following characteristics:

- *Conveys and strengthens the key points of difference or marketing messages for the brand/winery through every element of each guest's event experience.* In other words, the event is well-conceived from top to bottom, beginning to end;

- *Achieves the agreed-upon defined goals, which assumes that one has to have specific goals for an event before promising any sort of result.* (This may sound like the obvious, but we all know that events with ill-defined expectations happen — often.) Without this step, there will be no agreement on expected results, which can lead to misunderstandings and disappointment, usually on the side of management. Since most executives are not PR experts (and don't claim to be), it is up to us to do the educating;

- *Offers a fair return on cost for the brand or winery in terms of desired goals.* This is the "bang for the buck" part of the equation, which is more of a concern now than in the last 20 years in the wine industry.

I like to have comparisons for an event in mind in relation to other promotional options. Is the event equal in cost to an ad in the *Wine Spectator*? A national media tour of the winemaker? Sponsorship of a cooking show series?

Thinking about costs, payout, the tangible value of the event goals and making sure there is full comprehension among company leadership is time well spent. I should also mention that this doesn't mean the event is cheaply done by any means. It should reflect the quality and style of your brand and positioning, or be slightly above current brand perception (aspirational) if you are trying to raise perception.

What *are* the tough questions?

I have worked with a wide variety of clients over the years, as well as internal marketing teams and external agencies.

There is absolutely nothing else like the excitement one sees when a big event starts incubating. Results become easy to promise. *Everyone* will want to be there because it will be so fabulous! Budgets grow with the anticipation of results. There is excitement in the air as people begin imagining themselves at a lavish and well-orchestrated event, surrounded by "the media" (See first paragraph!), caterers swishing among the crowd with beautiful hors d'oeuvres... You get the picture. People get excited. People lose sight of realities of human nature, competition in the increasingly busy calendars of wine journalists, and sometimes even the realities of the media's perception or interest level in the winery/brand.

We unfortunately have to watch for the tipping over of the scale and be the voice of reality. There is a good reason for this, which I mentioned in the beginning: when the event is over, we are the people responsible for delivering all of the results that everyone has convinced themselves are so easy to achieve and practically a sure thing. We must be able to deliver.

So what are some of the tough questions that wine PR people must ask, internally first and then sometimes out loud?

- What exactly do we hope to get out of this event? What are the actions we want guests to take following our event? Are these expectations reasonable?
- How will we make the event unique to our brand/winery? Why will the media/the trade/consumers/wine club members come?
- Will the timing of the event make sense in light of our goals, other competing events, and the business (or media) cycle?

53

- Are we out ahead of an upcoming trend with this event, or following in a parade of similar events that might not be as compelling for media?
- Will the budget we have been given allow us to meet the desired goals, or is it unreasonable?
- Do we have adequate staffing resources for the event, and if not, can we secure an outside vendor?
- Is the management of the winery/brand able to host the event easily? Is it a good fit for him/her/them? (For example: Are you suggesting a black tie event for a vintner who is really only comfortable in jeans and cowboy boots? Is the event team expecting a shy vintner to become Johnny Carson for the evening?)
- If considering an outdoor event, is there a back-up inside location where the event can take place? How would moving it affect the quality of the event? What other logistical surprises might occur and are there ways to work around them?

Tips for making your wine event work

- Great wine events take place every week and continue to be one of the many useful tactics in every wine PR practitioner's toolbox. After the tough questions have been answered, how do you make your event a success? Here are some suggestions:
- Have at least three key goals. Agree on how event results will be measured as the event is beginning to take shape.
- Ask the tough questions listed above and make sure things are as much of a 'fit' for all involved as possible.
- Make the event compelling to media if that is your primary goal. Compare the value and anticipated results of a large event with other alternatives for garnering media coverage.
- Do research in the year prior to the event on what types of events are being written about and how. When you see a feature article, ask how it came to be if you know the PR person…connect the dots. Many features come from one-on-one pitching – not events!

- Get invitations out at least a month prior to the event if possible. Try to check the calendar for other wine events that might keep media from attending yours.
- Confirm and then confirm again. Make it tough for someone to cancel, but remind leadership that media (and other important people) *do* cancel.
- Last, but very important, involve multiple key audiences if possible so that you are diversified in your event investment. For example, create an event for trade, media and consumers so that you have potential benefits with more than one key audience.

***

Sara Cummings has worked in wine PR for over 20 years, and is currently Director of Marketing Communication for Sonoma County Vintners. Her background includes agency experience at Balzac Communications & Marketing in Napa, in-house experience as PR Director for Fetzer Vineyards at Brown-Forman, and for 14 domestic and international wine brands at Terlato Wines International. Reach her at winesara@gmail.com.

The Importance of Cause-Related Marketing in the Wine Industry

Kimberly Charles

In my 25 plus years in the wine industry, working in both the imported and domestic wine arenas on both the East and West coasts, I have been witness to the largesse of the industry – be it charitable associations, educational institutions, health related issues, and cultural endeavors among many other great causes. (According to the Wine Institute latest report of 2008, the wine industry contributed over $129 million to charitable causes.) The Business for Social Responsibility organization defines social responsibility as "achieving commercial success in ways that honor ethical values and respect people, communities and the natural environment."

The wine industry's connection to nature, coupled with the diversity of backgrounds of people working within the business naturally attracts people who are generous of spirit and who celebrate friendship, sharing and giving. Also, as it is a product created in nature, a synergy with agriculture and the effects it has on its communities naturally drives a sustainable farming philosophy, which is now the new baseline standard for wineries. Philanthropy is an organic extension of this philosophy and it has been and will continue to be a great platform from which to launch wine marketing programs.

It is important to note that creating a cause around a brand is not an end in itself. If a cause-related program does not help impact sales, it has failed. Oftentimes, public relations and marketing professionals can be overly excited about the merits of a creatively designed program, but unless it helps sell cases, it will be difficult to justify the investment in public relations. When a program is carefully crafted with both rational and emotional drivers, it can have more impact on sales than price incentives, advertising and other common tricks of the trade.

When executed well, these programs have resonance and impact when they truly connect with a brand's essence. Some recent statistics help support the notion that consumers respond to a well-thought program; today 79 perfect of adults would be likely to switch from one brand to another with a price and quality parity if the other brand is associated with a good cause compared to 66 percent in 1993 (Edelman PR). Two such programs are illustrated here representing a successful integration of either the brand's name and identity, the personalities behind the winemaking or the vision of the principals who owned the winery.

The Environment

Perhaps one of the biggest challenges the wine industry is facing in the 21st century is how to manage its role as a vital, growing agricultural business that inherently wrestles with environmental issues everyday in light of its water use, erosion control, herbicide/pesticide use, labor issues and many other elements that have an impact on the environment.

Recognizing this early on, Sequoia Grove Winery in Rutherford in Napa Valley, realized that raising the consciousness of consumers of wine about the need to preserve and protect our environment was of utmost importance. In the early 1990s, long before the sustainability movement had gained momentum within the wine industry, Sequoia Grove, together with its partner and marketer Kobrand Corporation, devised a program that targeted the restoration of trails in the Sequoia Kings-Canyon National Park in Northern California.

To put the program in context, it is important to note some of the challenges the winery was facing at the time. Its delicious estate and Napa-designated Cabernets and Chardonnays were receiving great accolades, however, the winery was competing with more established "big gun" names in the Rutherford district and needed a creative program to gain entrée into top accounts. Taking inspiration from the grove of majestic 100-year old Sequoia trees that graced the property, we designed a program that partnered with the National Parks and Conservation Program. The NPCA works on local, regional and national levels to help preserve and restore the national park system.

The name association of the park and the wine made it a clear connection with the brand, and consumers were asked to send in their Sequoia Grove corks to help restore the trails in the park. The program consisted of a campaign both on and off premise that described Sequoia Grove's involvement in the NPCA through shelf talkers, bottle-neckers, posters, menu cards and a full court press program.

It was such a "natural" fit that it caught the eye of the Hyatt Hotel group, who decided to make the program part of its national hotel restaurant campaign. The only hitch to the program was that the winery was inundated with corks coming back in the recycled envelopes provided. Such a headache to have! Today, some 20 years later the winery is still associated with the restoration and preservation of ancient Sequoia groves in California, a testimony to the strength of the campaign.

Health & Wellness

Ehler's Estate is a winery founded in Napa by Sylviane Leducq and the late Jean Leducq, who first purchased vineyard land in Napa in 1987. In 2001 they reunited the original 1886 Ehler's Estate vineyard and winery property by buying the remaining 30-acre parcel comprising the estate.

The Leducqs had sold their commercial businesses in 1997 and created a trust to benefit the Leducq Foundation, which supports cardiovascular research. Today it is the third largest medical research foundation in the world and the largest dedicated to one cause. Jean and Sylviane chose cardiovascular research as the focus as they knew it to be the leading cause of death worldwide and they wanted to help fund ground-breaking research to seek answers and solutions to this endemic problem.

A portion of the proceeds of the sales of Ehler's Estate wines go towards the foundation which as of 2010 had contributed over $187 million in funding to more than 105 institutions in 16 countries. The story is told simply on the back label of the wines and the design on the front label subtly reflects a heart symbol integrated into the "E" of Ehler's Estate. The integration and integrity of the Leducqs' philosophy and compassion into the winery's branding provides a great opportunity for a strong dialogue with the socially aware consumer.

A number of other great programs too detailed to elaborate here have met with success in the areas of scholarship, the arts and the welfare of those who support the wine community such as the farmworkers who are the backbone of the wine industry. It is all the more important for wineries to demonstrate to their customers a sense of consciousness, integrity and connectivity to a larger picture.

The future looks bright for the wine industry, leading the way towards more socially conscious enlightenment. Continued and generous charitable support, together with programs such as the Wine Institute's recent launch of the Certified California Sustainable Winegrowing certification, wherein close to 70% of the state's vineyards and wineries have evaluated their sustainable practices, are indicators that the wine industry has an opportunity to create a business model that other industries can emulate.

Making the Most of Your Trade Association Memberships!

Steve Burns

Of the more than 7,000 wineries in the US, almost everyone pays dues to one or more associations that are charged with the promotion of an appellation or publicizing a particular variety (ZAP) or a collection of varieties (Rhone Rangers). What's surprising to me is that most vintners fail to fully exploit these memberships to the benefit of their brand.

In the hyper- competitive sales and public relations environment found in America today, I would suggest that being actively involved in a successfully managed trade associations can provide more benefit to a wineries bottom line than an army of sales people or a high priced PR firm. What follows is a step-by-step account of how to ensure that your association is fully functional and that your membership dollars are not being wasted in that direction.

Do they have a plan?

One of the great conundrums of association management in the wine world is the pervasive lack of long term planning or even the basic possession of a long term (More than 5 years out!) strategic plan. Many association executives believe that they have a long-term strategic plan but what they usually have is a list of promotional tactics and "one off" programs without measurable parameters or applicable long-term goals and objectives.

Unfortunately, some associations with credible long-term plans fail to revisit them on an annual basis. What's even more troubling is the number of executive boards that allow their strategic plans to be "hijacked" by a market "blip" or an assertive (and often lone) vocal member with the proverbial "axe to grind."

This "tail wagging the dog" situation runs rampant in these associations, which sidetracks the associations marketing plan while greatly diminishing the value of your membership dollar.

For sure, it takes a substantial amount of fortitude on behalf of the board of directors and association executive staff to "stay the course," but isn't that their job?

What is success and what is their vision?

Having an agreed upon "definition of success" and a long-term vision is a vital part of any successful association's long-term strategic plan. Without these two pillars of measurability you would be unable to recognize success and when you have achieved it. These tools needn't be limited to a single parameter nor outlined in a fancy marketing plan but tactical short term *and* long-term measurement tools are a must. Media impressions, media coverage, membership satisfaction year-to-year, member sales results and even legislative victories are all applicable here. The most important things are, 1) benchmarking your starting point, 2) having measurable goals, and 3) measuring your achievements against those goals on a regular basis.

Do you have consensus?

The creation of any a long-term strategic plan is the responsibility of the association executive pure and simple. Having said that, the plan must be developed with the board of directors and key staff but everyone's job doesn't stop there.

The board *must* assist and back-up the association staff in building consensus around the plan with the association membership. One word of caution here: in all associations there are members who for some reason or another don't want to be part of "the team" despite the fact that they pay membership dues to a "team-like" organization. It goes without saying that these members must be heard and even met with if possible but they *must not* be allowed to derail the plan and slow down the association with their efforts. The association staff cannot do this alone; it's vital that the board of directors and key/larger members be engaged in the process of minimizing the impact of these members.

Begin to implement the plan (and stick with it!)

This is actually the easiest part of the process... Association staff or contractors can now begin to implement the long-term strategic plan on a tactic-by-tactic basis. Throughout the quarter, year or years of any plans implementation the board may/will be tempted by new promotional ideas influenced by changing

61

market forces but those "opportunities" should be reviewed every six months or annually rather than month by month to ensure program continuity. This will give the programs time to realize their potential and give the association staff the time to measure their results or lack thereof.

Keep the membership informed!

Second to actually having a long-term strategic plan, the lack of "Sell back" to membership is where most associations fail in their leadership duties. These days this communication can be simple, cost effective and a quick way using social media tools such as Facebook, Twitter and regular e-mail blasts. I see no need for an expensive and perpetually "out of date" four-color, printed and snail-mailed member newsletter. (Annual Report yes, newsletter no)

Enjoy the results of being located in a well-promoted AVA or marketing wines from a well-promoted variety or wine style!

Now the fun begins…"all of a sudden" key media want to take your PR pitches, distributors want to have your brand in their portfolios and most importantly you have lots of new customers and your existing customer base starts buying more wine!. Obviously all of this is not as simple as it sounds because I can name on one hand the number of successfully managed wine trade associations in the USA…but I won't!

***

Steve Burns was born in Germany and as is typical for an "army brat" he lived all over the world (Japan, Philippines and Washington DC) before his family settled in Half Moon Bay, Calif.

He attended California Polytechnic State University in San Luis Obispo because of the school's legendary "learn by doing" philosophy. With degrees in agricultural business management and animal science, he entered the world of agriculture as the northwest regional manager for the American Angus Association, coordinating all association activities in 11 western states. From 1984 to 1998, Burns was special assistant to Governor George

Deukmejian, participating in California's expansion in opening trade and investment offices around the world.

Since then Burns has become known in the American wine industry for his contributions as the Washington State Wine Commission executive director, serving from 1996-2004. He was concurrently the executive director of the Washington Wine Institute, the lobbying association of the state's wine industry. During his tenure in the Pacific Northwest, Burns started the America's first wine tourism taskforce that resulted unprecedented cooperation between the Evergreen state's two largest industries, which continues today.

In 2004, Burns created O'Donnell Lane, a marketing, public relations and strategic planning firm that specializes in association and non-profit re-alignment as well as board development and management.

Past clients include Sonoma County Vintners, Growers and Tourism Agencies, The Western Australia Wineries Association, The Oregon Wine Board, The Walla Walla Valley Wine Alliance, The Mendocino Wine and Tourism Boards as well as the Wine Institute of California. O'Donnell Lane is based in Sonoma County. Contact Burns at steve@odonnell-lane.com.

The New Public Relations

Social Media and Wine PR
Lisa Adams Walter

It was in late September of 2008 at the Web 2.0 Conference in New York City that I realized that everything in my profession had changed. I am a publicist. A wine publicist. A connector and a communicator. I'd heard the distant buzz about "social media" and suspected that, like the tidal wave that was the dawn of public access to the Internet in the mid '90s earlier in my career, something significant was about to happen. Five months prior, purely out of curiosity, I created my Twitter account. When I arrived at the Web 2.0 Conference, I hadn't tweeted very much –so I decided that I'd simply have to figure it out.

Silicon Valley publicist Brian Solis, a founding father of the PR 2.0 concept, spoke at the conference I attended that year. Solis is one who realized early on how PR, multimedia and the Web would intersect and create a new breed of PR/Web marketers.

Fast forward a few years, and it would now be rare to find a publicist who doesn't include social media as part of any communication campaign. What's the difference between traditional PR and the PR of today? There are similarities; there are differences too.

With traditional PR, we send out information. It's outbound PR. We still do that. Yet today we also work with inbound marketing. We position our messages and strategies so that our audiences can find out about us. Video, podcasts, fan pages, RSS feeds, apps and so on are all part of the New Media and viable and important PR channels for message dissemination. It's about the people we are trying to reach; it's about the public.

With traditional PR, we work with journalists. It's about building relationships and becoming a resource. We still do that. Yet, today the definition of a "journalist" is unclear. It's a debate too large for this brief overview chapter, but today's multi-faceted media includes: traditional journalists, journalists that blog, bloggers and citizen journalists – literally every person not just with a computer, but with a mobile computing device, now has the opportunity to "broadcast" from their "handheld computers" or smart phones.

So, I have worked hard to incorporate social media into every PR program in which I am involved. I believe in creating a strategy. To boil it all down for my clients, I advise that social media is simply one more channel – one more place to reach your audience. Why wouldn't you want your message out there? In addition to working the traditional PR channels, it's essential to work the new media channels too. The "sell" to clients is often a bit more difficult than it seems it should be. Not everyone "gets it!" In reality, however, it's pretty simple: social media provides a two-way street.

Brian Solis blogged some time ago in a post entitled, "I'm Not Talking to You," "Social Media continues to fascinate me…If you stop and think about it for a moment, we're presented with something special…something almost too simple to appreciate… essentially, we have been given a gift – a looking glass into the thoughts, opinions, feedback, and dialogue that represents a snapshot of market sentiment and behavior." Solis went on to say that the value of the gift is debatable. "It's time to shift from a mindset of monitoring and mining to one of collaboration, leadership, and justified adaptation. Give them something to talk about…"

That's what we do in Public Relations, we give them something to talk about. Traditionally, this is what PR pros do:

- Message development – tell your story
- Relationships with the media – properly gain interest in your story
- Repeat key messages until they sink in – via all channels
- The goal: editorial or "third party" coverage vs. paid advertising

With the addition of social media to the mix however, now more than ever, a huge part of PR is…

Listening. We now have the opportunity to listen, track trends and then respond.

Now that we are deeply engaged in the age of New Media, publicists have seen a monumental shift in our profession. The opportunities for message dissemination, which now is often instant, are massive. The new media is vast, hungry and eager to take messages and pass them on.

While PR has changed, at the core it's still about relationships. While a strategy is essential, more than 90% of success is based upon participation in the "conversation" – in other words, simply show up. While you are there, be yourself – or be your own brand. Establish a voice, identity and personality. Have fun!

Some examples of social media tools and platforms that can be used for PR include Twitter, Facebook, Blogs, Flickr, Help A Reporter Out (HARO), PitchEngine, Food Spotting and YouTube. Identify your audience and determine where they are. It's important to realize that the online community is just as tangible as customers standing in your winery tasting room. Rather than blatantly "sell," position your brand as a valuable resource that provides information customers want and need. Influencing perception is very different than selling. So, respect your online community and understand the importance of online reciprocity. If your friends and followers need promotion, give back to your online community too.

It has been reported that in mid-2011 approximately 140 million tweets appear every day while in excess of two billion Facebook "likes" and "comments" happen daily. The channels are out there. Audiences, potential customers and existing customers are listening and participating. There has never been a better time to tell your story.

***

Lisa Adams Walter has a diverse professional background spanning more than 20 years that includes PR, promotional marketing and writing experience in the wine/hospitality, entertainment, high-tech, publishing, pro sports and corporate environments. Adams Walter Communications, the agency she founded in 1999, focuses on public relations, social media, promotional marketing, writing and event management primarily in the areas of wine, food and the arts, using a broad range of tactics from traditional message development and dissemination, to the latest new media and Web 2.0 outreach techniques. Visit www.adamswalter.com, e-mail lisa@adamswalter.com or call (707) 255-0300 for more information.

Marketing to Millennials
Katherine Jarvis

Throughout the 1980s, Chuck Hope helped establish Paso
Robles' reputation for high-quality grape growing, with Hope
Family Farms and the family served as a driving force in the
development of vineyards throughout the region. These
vineyards became the primary fruit source for Chuck Wagner's
Liberty School brand, which the Hopes purchased in 1996. This
set the stage for the family's expansion from grape farming to
winemaking, under the leadership of Chuck Hope's son, Austin
Hope, who spent much of his time working in the family
vineyards from adolescence on through to adulthood, when he
became winemaker for Hope Family Wines. Today, the Hope
Family Wines portfolio includes wine brands Liberty School,
Treana, Candor, Austin Hope and Troublemaker. The Hope
Family portfolio appeals to a variety of consumers, from price
point to winemaking style, accounting for its national and
international appeal.

Austin Hope was instrumental in growing the Hope Family
Wines portfolio into the successful brands it is today thanks to
business acumen and a keen eye for what's hot in the
marketplace. Affable and magnetic, Austin also has a knack for
connecting with people – be they sales reps or consumers –
usually over his passion for music, outdoors, and having a good
time with wine no matter how expensive the bottle. He built a
reputation on the road for promoting – and pouring – Liberty
School as equally at home in Austrian crystal or in a party cup,
and for many in the industry, he epitomizes the ideals of an up-
and-coming generation of wine drinkers: millennials.

Austin feels passionately that connecting with millennials is key to
ensuring a future for family-owned wine brands, and to reach
young consumers it is necessary to embrace the world in which
they live. He set about creating a marketing plan to connect with
this essential audience on a platform, the iPhone, and medium,
music popular with young 20-and-30-something wine drinkers.
He then hired a Los Angeles-based advertising agency, 72 and
Sunny, to develop an iPhone application called "Wine DJ"

designed to create a custom streaming playlist of music based on the user's choice of mood, setting and Liberty School wine.

Austin hired Jarvis Communications in the summer of 2009 – just months before the app's launch – to create a media campaign focused on gaining both national consumer and wine trade press. Honing in on key influencers in each respective media market – music and technology, national lifestyle and consumer, and wine trade press – Jarvis Communications arranged a national media tour to bring Austin face-to-face with top journalists in each market. These included one-on-one meetings with journalists from publications including *Wine Spectator, Food & Wine,* and Reuters News Service.

To build as much buzz for the Wine DJ application as possible, Jarvis Communications also developed and planned pre-launch parties in New York and Los Angeles for wine media, as well as genres such as technology, music, lifestyle and consumer media popular with millennials. In New York, Austin walked journalists through the application, talked about the dearth of wines intelligently targeted to millennials and why Liberty School – a brand built on high-quality, well-priced wines – fits the sweet spot of price, quality and intrigue young wine drinkers seek, if only he could reach them.

The Los Angeles launch party was hosted in the warehouse-like space of the ad agency and featured demonstrations of the application, Liberty School wines and an introduction by Austin. Perhaps the most "buzz-worthy" part of the evening was the live DJ performance by local radio host and "indie" music celebrity of national renown, Jason Bentley.

Far from the typical staid wine dinners most industry reporters were accustomed to—and more hip, fun and slightly edgy than the typical "A-list" pomp and circumstance consumer media might have come to expect –both events were a huge success and resulted in considerable press. The parties went a long way toward bringing home the message that Hope Family Wines fit in perfectly with a new generation of wine drinkers, helped along by the staples of any good public relations program, of course: timely follow up, cordial communications, and access to the personality behind the story. Perhaps the best accolade for successfully portraying Hope Family Wines as a "cool" winery and principal Austin Hope as a "cool" guy was a story on hot young winemakers from Paso Robles featuring Austin Hope in *Details,* penned by a journalist who met Austin at the New York launch party.

Every good PR campaign leaves no stone unturned when it comes to potential audience and media influencers. While it may have been easier to stick within the boundaries of wine and music press, we felt there was a strong story in the Hope Family Wines choice to specifically target millennials by developing an iPhone app. By expanding our outreach to include not just national A-list press, but also marketing trades, technology reporters, and even entertainment media, we secured coverage in a wide range of diverse outlets including *Wine Enthusiast,* Variety.com, EntertainmentWeekly.com, *Zink* and intomobile.com, in addition to wine trade publications including *Market Watch, Beverage Media, Beverage Dynamics* and *Beverage World.* The resulting "halo effect" of our expanded outreach for the Wine DJ campaign continues to garner press for Hope Family Wines. The campaign allowed us to gain recognition from journalists who may not have noticed Hope Family Wines otherwise. Thanks to that positive association, we've been able to harvest continued media coverage for Austin Hope, Liberty School and other brands within the Hope Family Wines portfolio. and by staying in contact about other news happening at Hope Family Wines in the time since Wine DJ made its debut.

The Publicist and the Wine Blogger
Tom Wark

There was a time, not long ago, when the wine blogger was considered the pajama-wearing, basement-dwelling, poor cousin of the "wine writer." This perception of the wine blogger held by members of the wine trade, publicists and established wine writers derived primarily from the fact that there was no barrier to entry where wine blog publishing was concerned. Anyone with a computer and an Internet connection could set himself up as some sort of an authority. And they did. In huge numbers.

Yet the success of wine bloggers at drawing attention to themselves and their work and at creating an audience for their writing has dramatically changed the perception of the wine blogger. Today, many wine blogs are attract excellent readerships, contributing in substantial ways to the ongoing online conversation about wine and they are giving wine lovers considerable new options for wine recommendations and education:

Bottom Line: the wine trade and publicists ignore wine bloggers at their own peril and at the expense of good marketing efforts.

A short history of wine blogs

Self-published, on line "diaries" of the experiences and opinions of wine lovers began appearing around 2004. It was at this time when "blogging" was beginning to demonstrate its ability to grab the attention of opinion makers, search engines and consumers of information looking for alternative and regularly published information on their favorite subjects. Wine, as subject matter, was built for blogging.

Wine lovers love to talk, debate and discuss. The ease by which the blog publishing platform allowed wine lovers to offer up their opinions on wine and the wine world and the unique way by which blogs facilitate conversation nearly guaranteed that wineries, wine writing, the "best" wine, wine direct shipping, touring wine country and any number of other topics would find a home for discussion on this emerging platform.

But no one predicted the explosion in wine blogs that would occur over the next few years. At first a novelty, wine blogs eventually began to attract voices that had undeniable appeal and which began to attract substantial readers. By 2008 some estimated that nearly 600 wine blogs were being published on the Internet. No definitive count has ever been established, yet no one denies hundreds existed.

It was not long before the Wine Blog Awards emerged in 2007 and the best of the wine blogs were identified. In 2008 the Wine Bloggers Conference was founded convening in Sonoma County the first two years and going on to take place in Walla Walla, Washington, Charlottesville, Virginia and Portland, Oregon in subsequent years.

More and more "professional" wine writers also began taking up blogging, including Steve Heimoff of the *Wine Enthusiast*, Eric Asimov of the *New York Times*, Paul Gregutt, and numerous others who previously had published only in print and for payment. This migration of some of the best wine writers in America to a blog platform has done a great deal to legitimize the wine blogger.

Marketers and publicists were not quick to take note of this new contingent of primarily amateur wine writers, but in time the most forward thinking and keen observers of the wine media noticed that wine bloggers were attracting important readerships and presented opportunities to help tell their clients' stories. It is common today to see bloggers invited to press events, wine tastings, and media trips to far-off wine regions. By 2010, the wine blogger has become an integral part of the world wine writing and the wine media and savvy marketers and publicists are paying close attention.

Understanding Wine Bloggers

While the ever-expanding wine blogging community is now a full-fledged part of the wine media, certain characteristics set them apart and are important for publicists and marketers to understand.

Passion, not pay

The vast majority of wine bloggers receive no compensation for their efforts, either in the form of salary and fees or advertising and sponsorships. This makes their efforts driven primarily by a passion for wine, for writing or both. It also means that nearly all wine bloggers have a day job. All of this is important to keep in mind when reaching out to bloggers.

Skeptical of marketing

With so many wine bloggers having little or no journalism, public relations or professional writing experience, they have little experience working with or responding to communications with publicists. This results in a bit more skepticism of media relations and public relations than is possessed by the average writer or reporter.

No editor, no staff

Because bloggers almost always write on their own behalf, publicists will not be interacting with any editors or staff. It also means publicists need to appreciate an erratic or undefined publishing calendar. Finally, it means any interactions with bloggers will almost always be directly with the blogger themselves.

A down market focus

Regardless of the reasons, wine bloggers tend to focus on and review less expensive wines, rather than the rare, expensive, cult or high end wines. In some cases this is due to wine bloggers' tendency to work on behalf of the "average wine drinker". In other cases it is due to the fact that bloggers largely buy their wines themselves or have largely been sent samples of less expensive wines. Publicists should take these factors into consideration when choosing what kind of wines they choose to offer bloggers as samples.

Very social

Wine bloggers tend to use social media in a much more active way than the average wine writer. They use tools like Facebook, Twitter, Google+ and other platforms not only to market their commentary, but also to communicate, track what others are saying about them and to stay in touch with friends and colleagues. Publicists should be prepared to use these same tools when interacting with wine bloggers.

Readership

The total readership of wine blogs is notoriously difficult to come by, unlike wine magazines, daily newspapers and wine-related newspapers. The best known blogs obviously have better readerships. However, another way to gauge the readership of a blog is by observing the number of comments on various blog posts by different people.

Coming and going

It is the nature of blogging—it being so easy to launch a blog—that wine blogs come and go in a relatively frequent fashion. Some will last a year. Some last 6 months. A few last longer. Because few blogs are wed to income streams from the blog, it is quite easy to shut down the blog. Be prepared to see a favorite blog disappear.

A Publicist's Guide To Working With Wine Bloggers

Develop a list of serious wine bloggers

There are hundreds of wine bloggers on the Internet, yet only a relative few have a significant audience and post new content on a regular basis.

The publicist ought to set out to create a list of wine bloggers to follow and who will be added to their media list. Creating that list will take time and research, but it will pay significant dividends. And once the list is created its critical to watch the wine blog world for rising stars and new, important voices.

Understand the blogger's focus

Oftentimes bloggers will tend to focus on specific subjects. It's critical to understand the focus of each blogger. By doing so one doesn't end up sending a $40 bottle of wine to a blogger that writes about wine priced $20 or under.

Spend time reading the archives of blog posts on different blogs to get a clear picture of their focus. By doing so, you will prevent wasting your own time and the bloggers.

Query before sending samples

Many bloggers don't have regular tasting schedules. In addition, some bloggers don't accept samples. And in many cases, bloggers will note directly on their blog what their wine samples policy is.

It is always a good idea to note their policies before sending off a sample. And even better approach is to reach out directly to the blogger, briefly explain the wine you would like to send them for review and ask if they would like to receive it.

Appreciate blogger skepticism

Bloggers, as noted above, tend to have more skepticism when it comes to interacting with publicists and marketers than do experienced and professional wine writers who have become accustomed to being contacted by publicists. The best attitude to take into your outreach with bloggers is to appreciate their skepticism, listen to their concerns they may have with working with publicists, answer any concerns they have and, in the end, respect their skepticism if it persists.

***

Tom Wark is one of wine industry's most respected public relations professionals and considered one of America's top wine bloggers. Wark began his career in wine marketing in 1990 and opened his own public relations firm, Wark Communications, three years later to serve the communications and public relations needs of small and medium sized wine companies. In 2004 he started Fermentation: The Daily Wine Blog to voice his own opinions on culture, politics and society and how it all intersects with wine. Tom was honored with the Best Business/Industry Blog and Best Overall Wine Blog at the 2011 Wine Blog Awards. He is a frequent speaker on wine marketing, is often found at debates concerning the three-tier system, and continues to be a champion of wine bloggers and the wine blogging format. Tom lives in Napa Valley with this wife, Kathy, and an Italian Greyhound named Louis B. Shrimperton III.

How to Get Results from Virtual Wine Tastings
Rick Bakas

There were three virtual Australian wine tastings in March and early April that were a golden opportunity for anyone in the wine business. Wineries, sommeliers, retailers, importers and restaurants can realize ROA (return on attention) by following a few steps.

If you've never participated in a virtual wine tasting, the idea is simple—get a bottle (or bottles) of wine, taste and tweet along with other people at the same time on Twitter. The reason why you'd want to participate is to capture the attention of participants while it's happening. If the virtual tasting is planned properly, it's possible to have significant reach.

With traditional media, ad dollars are spent on reach. If we run an ad in a magazine, we're paying for the reach of that magazine. If we run an ad on television, we're paying for the reach of that station.

With new media, we can create our own reach through our fans and followers. When virtual tastings are orchestrated correctly, we can create a wide reach by bringing together an audience for a defined period of time. For #Cabernet day we had 3,000-5,000 participants who all had their own followings. If we average each person with a following of 300 friends/followers a conservative estimate for reach was 900,000 people (3,000 x 300). The upside is the community can scale up to an unlimited numbers. The downside is once the tasting is over, the community disbands. So we have to be ready to seize the opportunity. Here's some tips for maximizing the reach before, during and after:

1. Search the hash tag (listen)

Search for each hash tag while the virtual tasting is going on to "hear" what others are saying. Use Twitter Search, TweetDeck or kurrently to track the tag.

Personally, I like Twitterfall.com to put up on a monitor for others to see or TweetDeck on my laptop. I watch to see what others' experiences are.

2. Prepare content ahead of time (share)

Videos, blog posts, recipes or any other educational content can be created ahead of time, then posted during the virtual tasting. For example, during the #YarraWine virtual tasting wineries can do videos about their vineyards, soil or climate then post them during the virtual tasting. Because people are searching the hash tag, the content is likely to be seen by someone. You may even end up chatting with them real time during the virtual tasting to continue the conversation.

3. Share real time experiences

What wine or wines are you drinking? Share photos of the label, including the hash tag. Share your impressions of the wine, including the hash tag. For example, during the #HunterWine virtual tasting I'll interview winemakers in the Hunter Valley and post the short videos online during the tasting.

For wineries or wine shops wanting to sell wine, there are different strategies on how to make it happen before, during and after. Before any sales, coupons or offers can be made, there must be a level of trust with the online community. The worst thing anyone can do is start blasting out offers. If, and only IF the winery or wine shop is engaged with their community through lots of @ replies and one-to-one communications can they even think about selling anything.

If there's a healthy level of connection, then taste packs can be sold ahead of time. If a winery is hosting a virtual tasting, they can offer wines on-site at a promotional price. The most powerful use of new media is what happens after the virtual tasting. A savvy winery or wine shop will make the most of the opportunity and engage as many participants as they can. This is a targeted community of people who are participating –the community has already told us they like wine because they opted in to the tasting. Create Twitter lists or maintain communication with participants to grow the brand's own following.

Tweeting Bordeaux
Mike Wangbickler

There are few wine regions in the world that have a more traditional image than Bordeaux. The classic stories of chateaux, elegance and heritage have often made these wines intimidating to the average young consumer. In this evolving market, the Syndicat des Bordeaux et Bordeaux Supérieur wanted to reach out to these new consumers, and increase their reach in the American market.

The key was to update not only the message, but also the medium for the messaging about these wines. The less expensive and more approachable wines of Bordeaux and Bordeaux Supérieur are an ideal introduction to the world of Bordeaux, but to reach these new consumers, we needed to focus our efforts on conveying a fresher, more vibrant image of the wines and the region.

In terms of the messaging, it was critical to give more information on the way these wines are used every day in Bordeaux, and we did this with personal stories about the Bordeaux lifestyle and the next generation of Bordeaux winemakers. These winemakers are lively, energetic and fun…exactly the right people to change the staid image of more traditional Bordeaux.

But we also realized that approaching the same traditional wine journalists and critics who have written the same stories about Bordeaux year after year would not get us the results we wanted. More and more consumers (especially our target of Gen Xers and Millennials) are choosing to receive their news and information not from newspapers and magazines, but online from less traditional websites and bloggers. We needed to reach this younger and more open audience, and so we needed to work with these new media.

Along with a new interactive website and blog, we began to utilize social media tools (Facebook, Twitter, etc.) to promote the wines of Planet Bordeaux, the U.S. marketing program established to promote the wines of Bordeaux and Bordeaux Supérieur. One project, in particular, was a rousing success.

Working with a group of winemakers in Bordeaux and our Bordeaux-based counterparts at Vin'Animus, we put together a live virtual tasting using the Twitter network. This involved reaching out to a national list of non-traditional media, such as wine bloggers and those who write for electronic media such as Examiner.com, and inviting them to participate in a simultaneous tasting of the wines on-line. Expecting a handful of participants, we were delighted that our outreach generated an overwhelmingly positive response. We received requests from thirty –five different wine media and bloggers to participate in this event. We shipped wine samples to each participant in advance of the tasting, and provided them with information and contact numbers so they could follow along as we tasted the wines, live, with a live Twitter feed for all the participants.

The day of the tasting, a Balzac account executive along with participating producers in Bordeaux acted as hosts for the tasting, and each of the wines was tasted one by one. The media participants tasted the wines, posted comments on their impressions and asked questions of the producers in real time. The producers were focused on answering the specific questions about the wines, and our Balzac team focused on keeping the conversation moving in the right direction.

In the end, the back and forth communication became an invigorating exercise in controlled chaos. Questions, answers, comments and jokes all flew around the Internet, and for roughly two hours the wines of Bordeaux and Bordeaux Supérieur were the talk of the Twitter nation. Because of our flexibility and enthusiasm, the event created a very positive image of a modern style of Bordeaux wines and Bordeaux winemakers, and many the participants expressed how much they enjoyed the wines and the experience.

In the end, the media results were quite impressive. Not only did the 35 bloggers participate, but we had an additional 49 consumer "tweeters" join in the conversation. Although they had not received the wines, they were active participants in the conversation and added to the excitement. This clearly indicated that there was definite interest for the wines and that we generated some positive buzz within our target market.

In total we generated 1,088 "tweets" during the tasting, exceeding more than all previous tweets about Planet Bordeaux combined. Those tweets reached a potential audience of 184,052 people with 2,497,312 total impressions. And finally, in a more traditional method of measurement, over 15 of the media and blogger participants wrote about the event and the wines on their blogs.

In a two-hour time window, we were able to generate more buzz for Planet Bordeaux than ever before. The success of this event, and the buzz generated, allowed us to leverage that momentum in future communications with the participants and other non-traditional media.

***

Before moving to wine country, Michael Wangbickler knew virtually nothing about wine. Never one to shy from a challenge, he threw himself into learning everything he could about wine and the wine business by taking every class, reading every book, and tasting every wine he could. Mike now holds a Diploma in Wine & Spirits from London-based Wine and Spirit Education Trust and is a Certified Wine Educator. He currently holds the position of account manager at wine marketing and public relations agency Balzac Communications and Marketing in Napa, California and teaches wine classes on the weekends. In addition, he can often be found writing for his blog Caveman Wines where he offers advice on wine communications and marketing, conversing with fellow colleagues on Twitter, or contributing to discussions on any of the hundreds of wine blogs he frequents.

Case Studies of Wine PR

Opus One meets Maserati
Roger Asleson

It started with a fast-talking, super-slick voice-mail message from a marketing executive in Beverly Hills. In one run-on sentence, the message said something to the effect, "We represent J-Lo and Ben Affleck and Dustin Hoffman and Matt Damon and we have an incredible opportunity for you to get in bed with a premier producer of Italian sports cars," and "When do you wanna meet 'cause this is hot?"

After an obligatory recoil common in the wine business when promotions might combine drinking and driving, we called the fellow more out of curiosity than hope. He explained he was working as a go-between and didn't have an affiliation with any sports car company, and he didn't really know how we could work together, but he wanted to buy us lunch. A month later, the marketing whiz pulled up in mid-October of 2002 in front of Santa Monica's Chinois with a 2003 Maserati Spyder and an ingratiating smile.

We argued that any promotion Opus One did had to avoid being commercial, had to be managed with a light touch, had to be very tight logistically, and could not highlight a partnership with another business. It occurred to us that we were planning the next summer to host the successful bidder of the live lot Opus One donated in 2001 at the Napa Valley Wine Auction. The lot included the purchase of a 20-vintage vertical of double magnums of Opus One as well as a tasting and gala dinner for 20 guests, to be held on a mutually-agreeable date. Since Opus One had taken so long to deliver the tasting and gala dinner, why not sweeten the deal? Why not provide each of the ten couples who planned to attend these events with Maseratis for Wine Auction Week in June 2003? Though he lived elsewhere for most of the year, the successful bidder had also started his own small winery in the Napa Valley a few years before; he could certainly use some publicity himself.

We argued that the exposure from such a promotion would be beneficial to Maserati. But we also realized something was missing. Why not increase the exposure of the cars by including the Napa Valley Wine Auction itself? If a second group got the cars (perhaps the top bidders from last year's auction), the auction itself could offer more perks to this select group; more interest could be generated in the auction, the cars, and Opus One; Maserati could write off some of its expenses as an "in-kind" donation; and the auction's target charities just might benefit from the momentum. The directors of the auction and of the Napa Valley Vintners thought the same thing.

At length, Ferrari Maserati North America called back through its agency. They were still not terribly enthusiastic. They wondered how we could safeguard the cars when the drivers were slated, all week long, to attend one wine tasting after another. If we showed them a plan to provide limousines for the drivers after events in which wine was served, would they consider flying in from their New Jersey headquarters for a meeting at Opus One?

Yes, they would like to meet.

The head of the Napa Valley Wine Auction, the auction's director of communications and its chief PR consultant showed up promptly at the winery. Forty minutes later, four dark-haired men burst into the room with confidant smiles and perfunctory apologies.

We could work together, yes, but how could we provide for safety and maximize exposure of the cars?

If each driver, after an orientation and safety training by Maserati specialists, would sign a release accepting liability for damage to the cars, the deal was on.

Two days before the opening day of the Wine Auction, Opus One's bidder arrived with his wife and 18 excited guests for a photo shoot and safety orientation with the cars. In about an hour, they would also be treated to the 20-vintage tasting, attended by selected press as well.

The successful bidder owned a Citation 10 aircraft, so we arranged to bring this fastest commercial jet in the world into the Napa Airport. We would stage the jet with the cars for a photo shoot for an aviation lifestyle magazine. Japan Airlines caught wind of the photo shoot and offered its private hangar as backdrop for the shoot. Opus One agreed to provide a Japanese freelancer who would write up the event for a JAL in-house publication, and the deal was done.

Holding a well-known trade-only party the day before the auction, a wine magazine in which Maserati advertises could showcase the cars to yet another audience.

Before the cars passed to perennial top bidders of the Wine Auction, there were other uses for the cars: prior to the opening event, the auction arranged for the cars to be parked just at the entrance of the "Marketplace," the spot most visible to the 1,800 bidders and guests who would visit the lot display and barrel auction that day.

Held the night before the Auction, the Vintner's gala provided an orientation for the Maserati executives and another chance to showcase the cars. As busses drove the full complement of bidders and guests into the resort from remote parking, the cars were arranged just at the point where visitors debarked from the busses. That same night, the Ferrari Maserati executives attended the gala and were able to assess the audience's fit for the promotion. They were enthusiastic about coming back next year, but also acknowledged the need to do something completely different, if a return trip materialized.

At this writing, several articles are planned to cover these events. Several wineries have called Opus One hoping to get leads on doing similar promotions. And Ferrari Maserati reported two cars sold, in addition to prospective buyers who are currently negotiating the purchase of two additional cars.

***

Roger Asleson is director of public relations at Opus One Winery, a position he has held since 1995. Prior to his post at Opus One, Asleson held positions managing visitor programs at Robert Mondavi Winery. During that time, he acted as translator for Château Mouton Rothschild's Chef d'Equippe, who visited Opus One in 1985 and collaborated with Robert Mondavi to lay out one of California's first high-density vineyards. Asleson has also served for many years on the Napa Valley Wine Auction's PR committee. He lives in Yountville with his wife and daughter.

Free the Grapes!
Jeremy Benson

Free the Grapes! has attitude. The name of the consumer, winery and retailer grassroots movement has an exclamation point, and is symbolized by "Shackles," an illustration of a very, very mad grape. Shackles shakes his fist, he wants to be free, he demands attention!

The Free the Grapes! campaign appeals directly to wine lovers who, like Shackles, are mad about restrictions on their ability to purchase and enjoy the wines they want. In essence, our goal at Free the Grapes! is to channel consumer frustration over wine direct shipping restrictions into constructive action: letters to legislators, letters to editors, etc. The issue is now covered by over 200 news outlets each year, and includes a large consumer database and very active social media program.

The beginnings

Free the Grapes! first appeared on the scene in late 1997, formed as a result of an effort by the Wine Institute and the Napa Valley Vintners to defeat a bill in Florida that would raise the penalty for illegal interstate shipments from a misdemeanor to a felony. The bill passed, but the campaign generated a surprising amount of traction with consumers. An idea was born: to augment the legislative campaign to open up more states with a campaign that encourages the participation of consumer advocates. The campaign would provide a necessary constituency, consumer voters, in states where wineries have little political power.

Encouraged by the effort in Florida, the Wine Institute and Napa Valley Vintners joined forces with the legal team at the Coalition for Free Trade and other public policy groups, Family Winemakers of California and WineAmerica (known then as American Vintners Association), to establish Free the Grapes! A search was conducted and Benson Marketing Group was retained in May 1998 as its marketing, PR, Internet and administrative hub.

Thanks to a coordinated strategy, and the financial support of wineries, retailers and consumers, the direct shipping issue experienced unprecedented momentum in the mid 2000s. This was not always so, and we still have 16 states left to open, but we can't talk about Free the Grapes! without discussing how it fits into the industry's coordinated, three-pronged campaign.

First, Free the Grapes! handles PR and consumer outreach. Second, this campaign supports a national and state-by-state lobbying campaign spearheaded primarily by the Wine Institute, and with Family Winemakers of California and WineAmerica as well as a litigation campaign coordinated by Coalition for Free Trade.

As PR and marketing professionals, what are the main lessons learned?

Lesson 1: Coordination and strategic purpose

This campaign has been successful because leaders in the industry have focused on a single, coordinated, integrated campaign: PR, lobbying and litigation. PR has a purpose, a tangible result, and is therefore an integral component to the industry's strategy to allow consumers to purchase wines directly from wineries.

Many senior managers, however, don't understand how PR fits into their overall marketing campaign. As PR practioners it is incumbent on us to continuously educate and demonstrate the tangible results that PR delivers, to show visible proof of how PR and social media work together, and to reinforce the role that news coverage plays in marketing brands. Free the Grapes! is, after all, a brand.

Lesson 2: Sticking with a focused message

Free the Grapes! has used the following messages, repeatedly, ad nauseum, for years, and they have stuck:

"Wineries want to augment, not replace, the existing 3-tier system with limited, regulated, direct-to-consumer shipments." This statement is reasonable and logical, it is true, and it is threatening only to those who oppose direct shipping.

"A wine war is pitting consumers —who want to purchase wine directly from wineries —against wine wholesaler middlemen, who want all transactions to flow through their coffers." In other words, this is a consumer issue.

The wholesalers have attempted to complicate the issue; obfuscation can be a good strategy. We countered by simplifying the issue: can a consumer buy the wine he or she wants to enjoy, or not? Writers don't need to understand the dry complexities of the 3-tier system to understand injustice at a gut level.

Lesson 3: Integrated communications programs

Free the Grapes! is, at its core, a marketing communications campaign closely integrated with direct marketing and social media.

Our PR strategy has been to encourage wine writers to cover the story, but also to generate coverage in widely-read sections of newspapers: business, politics and news. We have reached a wide readership by moving issue into these sections as well wine columns and we keep our wine industry writers in the loop using a regular e-mail update when news warrants.

So through broad news coverage of the issue, every major newspaper has run at least one story on this issue. The catchy Free the Grapes! name attracts 20,000-30,000 consumers to our website each month. Once there, the site encourages consumers to sign-our e-mail list and engage in our social media program. We don't have the funds for an extensive print mail campaign.

Then, using e-mail and social networks, we inform our fans of pending legislation that we want to support or oppose. Our consumers can *easily and quickly* personalize a letter that is then automatically transmitted to the targeted legislators. We carefully monitor how many letters were written, to whom, and communicate regularly with industry lobbyists to ensure that our messages are on target.

Referenced organizations:

Free the Grapes!: www.freethegrapes.org

Wine Institute: www.wineinstitute.org

WineAmerica: wineamerica.org

Family Winemakers of California: www.familywinemakers.org

Napa Valley Vintners: www.napavintners.com

Wine & Spirit Wholesalers of America: www.wswa.org

Marketing the Health Issues of Wine
Theodore Berland

The fantastic press attention to the French Paradox did not just suddenly appear. Here is what was behind the news stories that happily declared the findings of a study that found that the hazards to health of a diet rich in fats—such as is consumed by the average inhabitant of Gaul—can be countered by a daily glass or two of wine, preferably red.

That publicity was built on a long-range program initially set in motion by the Wine Advisory Board, an agency of the California State Department of Agriculture. Its Medical Research Program modestly funded food scientists and medical scientists interested in investigating the ways in which the many components of wine beyond alcohol affected health. The aim was to fight with facts the negativism directed against all alcoholic beverages that was (and still is) generated by the drys in their zest to fight alcoholism. If successful, the positive publicity around these facts would also separate wine from other alcoholic beverages.

Over several years, a substantial body of scientific evidence accumulated to support the notion that wine taken in moderation is good for you. Telling the public of these findings then fell to the Wine Institute, the California wine industry's trade association based in San Francisco. After inviting presentations from more than 50 public relations agencies, it hired Daniel J. Edelman, Inc., to publicize this message [my words]:

Wine is more than a pleasant beverage. It is a complex natural fluid. Taken in moderation, wine promotes health and well-being. The benefits of wine, many known since antiquity, are now being scientifically confirmed. In short, wine is an elixir of life.

Edelman sent to San Francisco one of its key account executives, Harvey Posert, then New York office vice president, to handle the account full-time and on-the-spot. It also engaged freelance health writer Theodore Berland of Chicago to work and consult with the Wine Advisory Board's medical research director, Milton Silverman, Ph.D., and his successor, Salvatore Pablo Lucia, M.D., of the University of California-San Francisco Medical Center.

Dr. Silverman, previous science editor of the *San Francisco Chronicle* and, with his mentor, Chauncey D. Leake, Ph.D., past President of the American Association for the Advancement of Science, had co-authored *Alcoholic Beverages in Clinical Medicine.* This book presented the medical professions objective data on the values and contraindications of alcoholic beverages, including wine, in treating human diseases.

Dr. Lucia, a professor of medicine, had published, among other books, *Wine as Food and Medicine* and a *History of Wine as Therapy.*

Elements of the public relations program which Posert, Lucia, and Berland (with the help of Harry G. Serlis of the Wine Institute) constructed around the theme of wine as good medicine included the following:

Tastings of California wines presented at meetings of physicians and, especially, medical students. Along with instructions on how to taste wine, Berland offered at each tasting some facts about the health benefits of wine and passed out pamphlets that emphasized the point.*Studies of the use of wine in nursing homes, with the findings written by Berland under the name of each home's medical director and submitted to medical publications.*

Organization and execution of the International Symposium on Wine and Health, which was held at the University of Chicago's Center for Continuing Education. Leading researchers presented papers on their work on the values of wine given to patients and also participated in round table discussions. These were then published as a proceedings of the conference, *Wine and Health,* which was distributed to medical school and hospital libraries with accompanying publicity.

Organization of the National Study on the Medical Importance of Wine. The prestigious members of the Study traveled and worked in committees organized around topics. The committees met and wrote their findings as reports, which were gathered into a Final Report. Among the medical luminaries on the study was Morris Fishbein, medical columnist and former editor of the *Journal of the American Medical Association.* The final report was published to medical school and hospital libraries, with accompanying publicity.

These, then, were the building blocks upon which the French Paradox was built.

References

Leake, Chauncey D., and Silverman, Milton, *Alcoholic Beverages in Clinical Medicine*. Chicago: Year Book Medical Publishers., Inc., 1966.

Lucia, Salvatore Pablo (Ed.), *Wine and Health*. Menlo Park, CA: Pacific Coast Publishers, 1969.

Final Report of the National Study on the Medical Importance of Wine, 1971.

***

Theodore Berland is a Chicago-based freelancer, who has worked on PR campaigns not only for wine but also for cheese, meat, soup, medical, and pharmaceutical products; hospitals; universities; traditional and alternative medical schools and national associations. He has written 19 books and more than 200 magazine and newspaper articles; edited three magazines and seven books; and wrote a newspaper column on dieting for eight years. He can be reached at writer@ted-berland.us.

Seeking Long-Term Benefits: The American Harvest Workshop

Sara Cakebread

In the wine business, when the going gets tough, public relations is often asked to get going... right out the door.

As it is virtually impossible to measure case sales through public relations programs, and expected media results can require a rare level of patience, it is easy to dismiss the function as adding little or no value. However, if you can stay the course and maintain your energy and enthusiasm for a strong program or idea, the long-term effects might surprise you.

Every September for the past twenty-five years, Napa Valley's Cakebread Cellars winery has hosted its American Harvest Workshop, a culinary boot camp of sorts for chefs and journalists from throughout the country. For three days, an elite group of ten to twenty professionals immerse themselves in Cakebread Cellars' wines and foods from local purveyors.

For the members of the media who attend, it is often a whole new world as they are stripped of their pens and pencils and given a knife to pick grapes, a tool to peel potatoes for 150 or a bowl for foraging through the vegetable garden in search of 500 perfect cherry tomatoes.

Ideally, all the participants will take home with them a passion for what they have learned, along with a plan to add Cakebread Cellars' products to their wine lists, or a stack of notes to write a feature story that will appear before the last grapes of the season have been harvested.

Of course nothing short of giving the product away or having Brad Pitt endorse it will provide those kinds of results, but being patient and staying steady with a good idea can be almost as successful.

If the Cakebreads' event organizers were given the not uncommon directive to have five new wine list placements and three feature stories within six months, the program would undoubtedly be considered a failure and may never have made it to its second anniversary.

Yet as they celebrate their 25th anniversary, Cakebread Cellars has created a network of well over 100 top chefs from around the country who now have a fondness for this family-owned and operated winery. Though some may sell more wine than others, virtually all are eager to support them in any way they can. Whether it is hosting a winemaker dinner or using Cakebread Cellars products and literature for special events or by-the-glass programs, there is no doubt the relationships have proven to be fruitful.

Being that the Workshop is primarily trade-focused, it is even more difficult for the journalists who attend each year to respond with a story right away. Yet the media relationships that the winery marketing and public relations team has developed over the years have become invaluable. The hardest part for them is recognizing the need for patience when it comes to seeing the results of their publicity effort. A freelance journalist in New York who truly believed in the newsworthiness of the Workshop program once pitched the story fourteen times in almost as many ways before finding a home for it in a major lifestyle publication.

In the meantime, any one of the Cakebreads can feel comfortable calling on a Harvest Workshop media alumnus while traveling in markets around the country. Often this will result in a completely different story involving the winery but it will be "good press" all the same.

On the other side of the spectrum, representatives of the media know they can call on the Cakebread family when they have a need, often resulting in a quote, paragraph or photo in a major feature story. After meeting the people responsible for the entire range of functions at the winery during the early fall event, the journalists know they can always call Dolores Cakebread or Chef Brian Streeter to check a recipe or ask questions about the local purveyors, query Dennis about sales figures or the status of direct shipping in Texas or Ohio and look to Bruce and Julianne with inquiries regarding the vineyards and production. For virtually every aspect of a wine or food writer's work, there is someone at Cakebread Cellars who can respond, often a family member.

Recently, a major San Francisco newspaper featured Cakebread Cellars in a full-color, front page spread. An American Harvest

Workshop alumnus who attended the program several years ago when she was a writer for a Chicago daily wrote the story.

It may not be practical or financially viable to maintain a program for more than two decades regardless of the results, but if you and your superiors can be patient and stay the course with a good idea, the fruits of your labors should ultimately be in abundance.

***

Sara Cakebread is the owner of Telegraph Communication, a marketing communications firm whose specialty has been the wine and hospitality industries. She began her career with The Seagram Classics Wine Company in 1989, and as a member of the Cakebread Cellars family, has been immersed in the wine business since meeting her husband Dennis Cakebread at a wine event in Aspen in 1990. She is also a feature columnist for the local *St. Helena Star* and an active member of the community. Reach her at scakebread@comcast.net.

Kendall-Jackson Turns Adversity to Advantage
James Caudill

The plan was well thought out, or so it seemed. Advice had been sought, given and followed from experts at the local university, who briefed vineyard managers about regeneration, wildlife corridors and mistakes made in the past that should and could be avoided. Consultation had taken place with local community leaders and elected representatives. There would be no surprises, only support for a model vineyard development.

It didn't work out that way.

In the mid 1990's during a period of rapid vineyard expansion, Kendall-Jackson had already been singed —a sort of early warning alert —when it removed some oak trees during a vineyard development project in Sonoma County. Pulling oak trees from the ground made front page news locally, even as K-J's clean-up of nearby Sausal Creek, where old cars were pulled from the streambed and habitat was restored, didn't rate a word.

In Santa Barbara, rolling oak savannahs framing Highway 101 as it headed north were rapidly being converted to vineyards, not just by K-J but by several farming operations. Unfortunately, they tended to run together, and the impact of hundreds of acres being converted was far more visually dramatic as a result.

At the former Barham Ranch, dotted with more than 10,000 oak trees, Kendall-Jackson planned to develop less than half of the land, leaving most of it in open space, a needed rest from over-grazing by cattle historically found in these canyons. For the 600 or so acres that would be planted, an average of 1.5 trees per acre would be removed, and all would be replanted at a ratio of 10 trees for each one taken, grown on-site from acorns nurtured to seedlings, then irrigated for several years until safely rooted. Wildlife corridors would run through the vineyards, allowing free and easy passage for native animals heading toward water. Rubber-tracked vehicles would be used to lessen the potential for erosion.

When the bulldozers began developing the vineyard, drivers on the nearby highway didn't see Kendall-Jackson's careful plan.

They weren't individually briefed on restoration. Instead they saw nearly 1,000 trees taken from the ground, piled high in burn piles to dry and be disposed of after salvageable wood was removed. An environmental firestorm erupted, and everyone in the industry began to realize that vineyard development would never occur easily or without oversight again.

It was a perfect public relations storm. Before it was over, waitstaff in restaurants boycotted K-J wines, refusing to serve customers. Lawsuits were filed by local environmental groups (which, for the record, K-J later won since it had carefully followed all rules and regulations then in effect), elections were held to stop the cutting of virtually any tree, and even recall campaigns were launched against local officials, regardless of which side of the issue they were on.

Wineries had always seen vineyards as beautiful open space, the last bastion of agriculture that would save land from conversion to subdivisions or development as strip malls and tacky suburban excess. Most vintners were stunned, and none more than Kendall-Jackson.

As the grow tubes went in to protect the young plants, vineyard managers could look ahead and visualize a verdant green oasis, watched over by raptors drawn to the roosts and owl boxes K-J provided. But in the Los Angeles Times, one local resident described a different scene. Where vineyard managers saw future beauty, she said the carefully aligned rows of tubes and milk cartons resembled nothing so much as a national military cemetery, symbolic headstones for a lost ecology that had been disrupted for a product seen not as food, but as sin.

Public relations should have done a more complete job in understanding the potential visual impact of the development, and helped craft a more detailed plan to gain understanding, if not support. The Internet as a briefing tool was only beginning to be effectively used. But public relations was going to be the only effective way out of the growing morass, with Kendall-Jackson now seen as a lightning rod for environmentalists opposed to vineyard expansion, and regularly charged with evils large and small, mostly built on fabrication, exaggeration or a skewed view of the facts.

In this atmosphere, fighters within K-J wanted mostly to fight. There was a champion for careful, rational action, however, and the value of seasoned leadership was never more proven than in the response that was crafted.

Kendall-Jackson co-founder Barbara Banke set the tone and direction that would change Kendall-Jackson's fall from grace into a new opportunity for understanding and cooperative effort.

Having followed all regulations, Kendall-Jackson had done nothing technically wrong. In fact, having sought out assistance to plan a model vineyard that would feature restoration and protection in more than equal measure with development, there was a good story to tell. Rather than apologize, K-J began to communicate.

Phone calls, letters and e-mails came in regularly and every single one was answered personally with a review of what had actually been undertaken and accomplished. One exchange with noted wine critic Hugh Johnson was famously published in Harper's, a British wine trade magazine. After hearing a more complete report, he wrote a personal note saying he wished he'd not been as hasty to criticize as he had been. Local reporters were briefed and briefed again on the original plans, and how the plans were being put into action. By responding quickly to media inquiries, the strategy was not to let the story grow faster and further, becoming a national *cause celebre*.

Contact was made with the California Oak Foundation —one of the loudest critics of the winery —and the executive director agreed to come to the ranch and hear the story first hand, making her own journey of discovery. From that early contact grew cooperative efforts which found Kendall-Jackson working to underwrite additional oak research, conduct oaks in the vineyards workshops for opinion leaders and support educational outreach on oak restoration to California school children and elected officials.

Foundation officials helped Kendall-Jackson construct a carefully considered pledge not to cut endangered species of oak trees, and to continue restoration efforts on its own ranches, and to support similar efforts underway throughout the state.

A review of farming policy led Kendall-Jackson to announce, to the astonishment of many present at a meeting of the Sonoma County Growers Association, that it would not only no longer cut trees in vineyard development, but that it was banning the use of methyl bromide and several other pesticides that threatened groundwater. While many others were also following such policies, none had stepped forward to say so publicly. While not seeking the spotlight, Kendall-Jackson suddenly found it, being cited by environmentalists not as the evil empire but as an example of an enlightened grower capable of consulting with, and responding to, community needs.

At the same Barham vineyard, where controversy once reigned supreme, visitors from government, environmental groups and other vintners now come for visits to see, finally, how careful planning could allow for a vineyard development that would support and enhance the environment. Oak seedlings have been catalogued and followed through regeneration, and a vibrant eco-system exists.

When the United States Environmental Protection Agency awarded a series of Stratospheric Ozone Protection Awards in Washington D.C., there were two wineries among the honored from industries and organizations throughout the world. Fetzer Vineyards, long known for its sustainable business practices and leadership in organic farming, and Kendall-Jackson, a once unlikely partner in environmental leadership, were cited as an example of good stewardship.

A simple public relations premise and a courageous leader carried the day.

The public relations lessons are easy to tell, but carrying them out, particularly in a highly charged atmosphere, is anything but easy.

Don't run, you can't hide: *communicate.*

Tell your story. Carry the story forward. Don't let it carry you.

Keep the conversation going, even if it hurts.

Listen well, and learn.

Allow yourself to get caught in the act of doing something good.

***

Jim Caudill served as vice president, public relations & hospitality for Kendall-Jackson Wine Estates during a period of rapid growth and controversy. As a wine industry consultant, he has represented wineries large and small, and served as director of trade public relations for Brown-Forman, before accepting his current position as director, public relations & hospitality for Hess Family Estates. He is a Fellow of the Public Relations Society of America and a three-time winner of the Silver Anvil, the Oscar of the public relations industry. After a career as a journalist, he served as a top management consultant for several major public relations agencies, including Carl Byoir and Ketchum Communications, and as vice president, public relations for Amfac Hotels & Resorts. Contact him at JCaudill@hesscollection.com.

Building a Name for Lodi
Mark Chandler

Imagine yourself with a client whose products had provided consumer satisfaction for decades and who was once considered a leader in its industry. Imagine that this client lagged in its response to market trends and as a result its reputation became tarnished, even maligned. Although in time your client would make the appropriate changes, its current reality was largely misunderstood or ignored.

That was the situation for Lodi winegrowers when I became Executive Director of the Lodi Winegrape Commission in 1991.

At the time the large wineries knew that the quality of Lodi grapes enhanced the character of their California appellation wines, but only a few small wineries were producing "Lodi" appellation wines. Despite the fact that the early California wine trade was centered in Lodi, a whole generation of winemakers considered Lodi a viticultural backwater, and grower prices reflected it.

The region's reputation needed a serious facelift. We set out to increase demand for Lodi winegrapes by expanding the base of client wineries, and to increase the number of wineries in Lodi. To accomplish this, a trade PR campaign was envisioned, with the target market being winemakers, grape buyers and CFO's. We could deal with consumers later.

Our message was clear – due to our Northern California location, our cool climate influenced by San Francisco Bay breezes, and our innovative growers, we could produce great fruit at great prices. This fruit could be used either in Lodi appellation wines, or it was perfect for blends designed to satisfy the growing, thirsty market of the mid-1990's.

The knock on Lodi was part image, part reality. To deal with the image problem we developed the PR campaign. To deal with the reality, we initiated a series of Quality Enhancement Seminars. Local and coastal winemakers shared their Lodi wines with growers in a classroom tasting format, offering advice as to how the region could improve quality. Steadily, quality has improved.

The image enhancement campaign started with an eye-catching logo and first-rate graphics for press packs and ad campaigns. Those images convey a contemporary feel and imply quality in everything we do.

Our first trade magazine ad campaign, "Six Grape Reasons to Buy Lodi Grapes," featured the region's climate, quality, dependability and blendability as inducements to buy Lodi grapes. Later we refreshed the campaign through an innovative reformatting, running a series of 1/3-page vertical ads sideways on successive right facing pages. You couldn't help but run across them, no matter which article you were reading.

To consolidate the message about our Northern California location and cooler-than-Central Valley climate we ran the "Location, Location, Location" campaign. This ad featured a map showing the cool breezes off the San Francisco Bay heading toward Lodi, and that little ribbon of Highway 12 starting in Santa Rosa, wending its way across southern Napa and on into Lodi.

Perhaps our most successful campaign was the "Zins of Lodi," where we reproduced any label of Zinfandel bearing the Lodi appellation, free of charge to the winery. Every time we ran it more wineries would call up demanding to be in the ad, since they too had a Lodi Zinfandel. We would insert their label into the ad, paying additional artist fees each time, of course! The 13 original labels were joined by some thirty-plus, and the ad became a two page layout instead of the full page that was originally designed (and budgeted for!). Today this would take up even more space, as there are over 60 Lodi Zins in the market. It was a great campaign with a great result.

Another successful campaign was "Lights are Shining on Lodi wines," which listed quotes about Lodi from notable wine writers. It demonstrated that Lodi is not just about Zinfandel anymore, and that some very knowledgeable voices are chiming in on the Lodi tune, from Dan Berger to Robert Parker and others.

"Great Wines from Real People from a Great Place" became our next motto and campaign theme. It reflected the authenticity of the winegrowers and helped create a sense of place for Lodi.

To carve out a niche from a PR perspective, a region has to be known for some one thing, or a very few things, that can help shower a positive impression on all the other things it does. For us Zinfandel was a great launching point, in terms of wine. It focused on one of our strengths, something we did well.

But as to *winegrapes*, I remember early on struggling with one core question – how do you add value to grapes *in the field* (a lot of grapes, not just Zinfandel)? It wasn't long before I got my answer, when one of our growers suggested a district-wide Integrated Pest Management Program.

This program was not launched simply as a PR exercise. It reflects grass roots community values – respect for the land and respect for the workers in the farming operation. It was designed to help growers deal with the ever more burdensome regulation of agricultural chemicals by reducing the use of synthetic pesticides. It has succeeded in those areas, as well as creating a positive image for Lodi vineyards.

Our viticultural leadership was further consolidated with the publication of the "Lodi Winegrower's Workbook" in 2000, authored by our own Dr. Cliff Ohmart. It was the first comprehensive guide to viticulture published since Winkler's text in 1974! It became the primary source for the standards used in our "Lodi Rules for Sustainable Winegrowing." This is the industry's first third-party sustainable certification and sets the gold standard for other certifications that have followed. These programs allow the wine industry to wear a white hat with regard to the environment. Our leadership in this arena has benefited the entire California wine industry, and has helped establish credibility for the Lodi region, its grapes and its wines.

The Lodi Wine and Visitor Center is another idea designed to increase our visibility. The 7000-square-foot center, which opened in Fall 2000, contains numerous displays on grapes and wine, complete with a retail room offering some 200 Lodi wines for tasting and sale. The center has hosted hundreds of wine industry leaders at dozens of events, as well as tens of thousands of visitors from around the world. As with any good tasting room operation, we have a wine club so that enthusiasts from around the country can enjoy their quarterly selection of Lodi wines.

Lastly, so much of good PR today is having an engaging and accurate website (ours is lodiwine.com), as well as a social media program. We have added staff to help extend our message in the cyberworld.

Have we succeeded in our mission? By many measures the answer is a resounding "yes."

In the media and the trade, we have literally changed geography, as Lodi has become a standalone region, rather than being categorized with the Central Valley.

We have legitimized Lodi as a source of high quality grapes and wines. We now have 85 wineries in the appellation, ten times the number when we started, with dozens more around the state buying Lodi grapes. There are now 450 Lodi appellation wines in the market, where there was a mere handful before.

We have generated numerous feature articles in the wine media and entertained top wine writers here in Lodi, a prospect that was unthinkable in the not too distant past.

From a mere trickle there is now a cascade of medals being showered on Lodi wines at all major wine competitions - so many that the California State Fair created a stand-alone category for Lodi, rescuing it from the anonymity of "other regions."

And we have a magnificent center to entertain wine enthusiasts and media alike.

Every label, every award, every visitor, every story in the press builds on the momentum we started twenty years ago. Perhaps wine writer Dan Berger expressed it best in an article in the *Napa Valley Register*, "One of the most difficult things to do in this world is change a reputation, but the Lodi wine grape region is doing just that."

***

Mark Chandler is a seventh generation Californian with a passion for enhancing the role of wine in American culture. He holds a degree in Agricultural Business from California Polytechnic University, San Luis Obispo, and is a graduate of the esteemed California Agricultural Leadership Program. In his 30 years in wine he has been a winemaker, marketing manager, wine educator and vineyard owner.

Chandler was executive director of the Lodi (CA) Winegrape Commission from 1991 to 2011. Under his leadership Lodi's star has risen on the California wine scene, with the number of wineries increasing from eight to 85. The Lodi region has also become a world leader in sustainable viticulture.

Chandler is past president of the Society of Wine Educators. He is a Supreme Knight of the Brotherhood of the Knights of the Vine, and was named *Sunset* Magazine's "Wine Professional of the Year" in 2005. He is a judge at several national wine competitions and a frequent speaker at wine venues around the globe. Contact Mark Chandler at Chandler & Company 1900 Edgewood Dr., Lodi CA 95242, (209) 481-0848 or mark@markhchandler.com.

Building a Brand, Creating a Category
Gino Colangelo

The background

In 2000, after once unsuccessfully trying to enter the US market using only an importer, Mionetto SpA, one of Italy's most progressive Prosecco producers, made the decision to invest in its own American subsidiary and opened Mionetto USA. Unable to attract the attention of the right distributors with a sparkling wine almost completely unknown in the US, Mionetto got its own distribution licenses in the New York tri-state area. So with a staff of one, a limited marketing budget and a little known wine variety from somewhere north of Venice ("Valdobbiadene?") Mionetto hired my agency and set out to build a wine empire in the US. All of the investment and the risk – as well as the potential reward – would be entirely their own.

Mionetto and my agency team didn't lack challenges.

First order of business: Make the American wine trade, followed by America's wine drinkers, aware of Prosecco. In 2000, even many wine writers had little or no knowledge of the variety.

Secondly, educate Americans about sparkling wine: sparkling wine is not just Champagne, and you can drink sparkling wine every day (it's not just for New Year's Eve and weddings).

Finally, calibrate brand awareness with distribution. Translation: don't waste precious marketing capital in areas where Mionetto didn't have wine available to purchase. So the PR plan had to roll out in perfect alignment with the distribution.

Being optimistic (a useful trait in the public relations business), the Mionetto agency team saw some opportunities as well.

Prosecco has great taste characteristics for America's casual wine drinkers: fruit forward, slightly sweet and not too complex. And Mionetto makes very palatable Prosecco.

Prosecco is from Italy, a nice advantage for an imported wine given America's ongoing love affair with all things Italian.

Prosecco is right in the sweet spot price-wise with most Proseccos, selling from $10 - $15, and Mionetto fit this price range.

Prosecco is easy to pronounce (even if Val-doh-be-ad-di-nay isn't).

Most importantly, Mionetto was the first Prosecco brand in the US with a sustained, agency-supported, focused communications program allowing us to own the Prosecco story for Mionetto (at least for awhile).

The public relations program

The goals were, in this order:

Build the Prosecco category in the US

Make Mionetto synonymous with Prosecco

Support sell-in to trade and pull-through with consumers in focus markets

Based on focus groups and given the style of wine, we determined that the primary consumer audience for Mionetto Prosecco would be largely female, casual wine drinkers who enjoy a conversation *with* a glass of wine, not *about* a glass of wine.

Next we established the brand positioning (simple but effective):

Mionetto, *the* Prosecco

The positioning was supported by the tagline, "No Occasion Required."

We developed the key messages to support the positioning and communicated them consistently in every communication and target audience interaction: In written and verbal pitches, interviews (through media training with the Mionetto executive spokesperson), at events (by training sales promoters) and all other trade and consumer touch points. The messages:

- Easy to drink (rounder, softer bubbles than Champagne)
- Unpretentious
- Affordable (alternative to Champagne)
- Versatile
- Social

105

- For everyday consumption

The core of the plan was media relations. Italian wine trend stories, sparkling stories, features, business stories, pairings, occasions for drinking: we pitched them all, assiduously sticking to the messaging and careful to follow distribution as Mionetto rolled out nationally. The breakthrough story was in the *New York Times* not long after program launch: "It's the Fizz This Summer (And It's Not Champagne)," by Amanda Hesser, *New York Times,* July 11, 2001.

The buzz with media snowballed from there, following the adage, "If it's a story for the *Times*, it's a story for me."

As with any (quality) wine, sampling was critical. We did consumer and trade events, product sponsorships, product placements — lots of leg work and pouring product with low cost on the sponsorship dollars. Given the limited resources, we encouraged the client to be generous with product. Especially in the wine category, if you believe in what you're pitching, always lead with product.

We executed a limited advertising plan to achieve two objectives: demonstrate support to the trade and create pouring opportunities at media-driven events. Every dollar spent had to achieve multiple goals.

We held a Prosecco pairing cook-off (to reinforce the every day drinking/pairing message) where participating chefs could either use Mionetto Prosecco as an ingredient or pair Mionetto with an original dish. Winning trip: to Venice and Valdobbiadene.

As the program evolved we targeted bartenders and held cocktail contests (Prosecco is a great mixer), wrote releases on picnics, weddings (Prosecco as an alternative to Champagne) and home parties — any and all potential occasions for drinking Prosecco.

Mionetto brand awareness quickly became greater than actual sales and distribution. We struggled with the challenge of the communications moving faster than distribution as Proseccos with more established distribution — namely Zardetto and Nino Franco — were realizing the benefit of Mionetto's marketing investment. Ultimately Mionetto was able to build a national sales organization which leveraged the brand awareness into sales, which resulted in Mionetto establishing itself as the Prosecco market leader in the US, a position the company still holds today.

Where Mionetto is today

Mionetto is the Prosecco category leader with 34 percent market share. The Prosecco category is growing 42 percent while Mionetto is growing 41 percent, pretty heady numbers for any brand or category.

Mionetto's challenge today is to maintain category leadership in the face of much savvier, better funded competitors like Gallo and Palm Bay. To answer this challenge, Mionetto is now focusing on more mass consumer branding mainly through social media and Web marketing, which fits the Prosecco demographic and Mionetto's still modest marketing budget.

***

Gino Colangelo is President of Colangelo & Partners Public Relations in New York. He founded Colangelo & Partners Public Relations (www.colangelopr.com) in 2006 after spending over 10 years with Dentsu Communications, where he pitched and won new business, and conceived and put into play communications strategies for a great client list that included Siemens, Olympus, Japan Airlines, Finmeccanica, Suntory, Winebow, Mionetto and lots of others. Before Dentsu, Gino spent 10 years in his own retail business, a unique experience in the agency world. Prior to the retail business, Gino spent 2/1/2 years in Japan writing copy for an ad agency and writing freelance for travel magazines. He has also lived and studied in Siena, Italy.

Gino's love of food, wine and spirits has led to CPR's focus on these "worlds of passion." The Colangelo & Partners client list includes: Marchesi de' Frescobaldi, the Soave Consortium, Folio Fine Wine Partners, Vinitaly / Veronfiere, Partida Tequila, Grana Padano PDO, Kusmi Tea, Asiago PDO, Speck Alto Adige, Luce delle Vite, I Spirit Vodka, d'Alessandro Wines and many others.

Reinventing the Wheel: A Case Study From Beringer Vineyards

Mora Cronin

One of the biggest challenges facing wine marketers and publicists in the U.S. is how to make wine more accessible and understandable to consumers without entirely eliminating the mystique that has made it such an interesting and enduring beverage. There's no doubt that the plethora of labels, the complexity of vintages and appellations and the sheer enormity of the subject matter have scared many consumers away—people who think (and who can blame them?) they need to "know" something about wine to drink it.

As more Americans became acquainted with premium varietal wines in the 1980s and 1990s, some of the barriers to wine enjoyment became more apparent. At Beringer Vineyards, many of the questions we received from consumers revolved around how to describe the wines they tasted. While simple descriptors such as "light," "mellow," or even plain old "good" were fine for beer or mixed drinks, consumers seemed to believe that more descriptive terms were required when talking about wine.

And no wonder! Back labels as well as wine reviews were filled with terms such as cassis, mint or chocolate, leading some consumers to believe that fruits, vegetables, herbs, spices or other flavorings had actually been added to the wines. And some critics took great creative license in ascribing personality traits to wines, using words such as "cheeky," "classy" or "charming." These terms might have meant something to a seasoned wine drinker, but to a novice they simply added to the confusion. "I like this wine but I'm not sure how to describe it," was the plaintive cry heard from many consumers.

In 1997, a team led by Beringer's Director of Sensory Research at the time, Jane Robichaud, decided to address the issue of consumer uncertainty and intimidation. The team created the "Beringer Wine Tasting Wheels," a set of two wheels —one for white wines and one for reds —designed to help wine drinkers identify, remember and describe the common aromas and flavors in red and white wines. Robichaud, who ran Beringer's research winery, was the perfect person to lead the project. As a graduate enology student at the University of California at Davis, she had worked with Professor Ann C. Noble on the original Wine Aroma Wheel, a tool for professionals looking to identify the most common aromas —both desirable and undesirable —found in wine.

"While terms such as ethyl acetate and butyric acid might be useful to the student winemaker, they're not really that helpful to a consumer," said Robichaud. "Our idea was to put the basic vocabulary of wine at people's fingertips. When you have a list of potential terms in front of you, it's much easier to describe a wine than when you're trying to pull adjectives from thin air."

To accompany the Wine Tasting Wheels and help people understand how to use them, Robichaud developed a sensory seminar adapted from a training class she was using with Beringer employees on how to taste and evaluate wine. Robichaud created "aroma samplers" using neutral white or red wine mixed with food products such as a piece of vanilla bean or a dash of ground black pepper, for example, to imitate the aromas most typically found in wine. Participants would "sniff" through a dozen or so samples to become familiar with, and comfortable describing, these common aromas.

"This is a really straightforward way of introducing people to the language of wine," commented Robichaud. "Many of the aromas and flavors found in wine come from groups of compounds that are found all over the natural world, in fruits, flowers, herbs, and of course, wine grapes. Others, such as butter or vanilla, are the result of techniques used by the winemaker. Isolating these aromas in a seminar like this helps people to pinpoint and remember them more easily."

Armed with the Wine Tasting Wheels, the seminar, and the effervescent Robichaud as a spokesperson, the Beringer public relations team went to work. The goal was threefold: 1) to help consumers feel more comfortable with wine; 2) to create a halo for Beringer Vineyards as a leader in the field of wine education and a friend to the wine consumer; and 3) to build brand loyalty and awareness of Beringer Vineyards wines.

Two "Come to Your Senses" press events were held in New York: one for food, general interest and women's media outlets, and one for wine writers and critics. At each event Robichaud led an interactive sensory seminar tailored to the audience, showcasing Beringer wines and introducing the Wine Tasting Wheels. Each seminar was followed by a meal prepared by Lespinasse restaurant, accompanied by Beringer reserve and older vintage wines. The reaction was immediate: the "general" media audience, although sophisticated New Yorkers, had the common lack of confidence about their wine knowledge, and the editors commented repeatedly about how much fun they had and how Robichaud's program took the "scare factor" out of wine tasting. The wine writers, expert tasters already, were pleased to get a take-away they could offer to their readers.

Immediately following the events, the PR team developed four separate media mailings for wine, food, lifestyle and general interest press nationwide. The press kit (also distributed at the press events) included the Wine Tasting Wheels, a press release about their development and how consumers could order them, as well as step-by-step instructions on how consumers could give a simple wine tasting seminar, complete with aroma samplers, at home.

Media coverage of the Wine Tasting Wheels was widespread and overwhelmingly positive. Within three months, the Wheels had been featured and offered to consumers in dozens of publications, including *New York* magazine, *USA Today, Wine Spectator* and others, as well as the TV Food Network. The estimated audience reach during that same time period extended into the millions, and the winery fulfilled over 4,000 requests for the Wine Tasting Wheels from consumers all over the country. In the years since, and even in the absence of any focused public relations effort, the Wheels continue to generate publicity "pops" here and there, and consumer requests are received on a steady basis. Now in their third printing, the Wine Tasting Wheels have been distributed to over 15,000 people in the U.S. and throughout the world.

Importantly, the Wine Tasting Wheels also became a useful tool for the trade, and reinforced Beringer's leadership position in the wine industry with this key audience. The winery's sales force used the Wheels in seminars and training sessions with restaurant wait staffs, retailers and distributor sales forces across the country, ultimately ordering so many that they needed to be reprinted within six months of their introduction. The Beringer Wine Tasting Wheels were also made available to consumers at the winery and via the winery's website.

Perhaps the greatest testaments to the success of this program were two events that occurred within a year of the Wine Tasting Wheels' debut. First, Robichaud was asked to lead a sensory seminar for the Smithsonian Institution in Washington, D.C., a rare invitation and opportunity to deliver Beringer's messages to another intellectually curious audience. Second, in the fall of 1997, Robichaud was honored by *Food & Wine* magazine as one of eleven "visionaries" who the magazine said were changing the world of wine. As the editors put it, Robichaud received this top honor for –what else? –"reinventing the wheel."

***

Mora Cronin is a consultant who specializes in marketing communications, copy writing and public relations services to the wine industry. Until 2005 she served as Vice President of Public Relations and Corporate Affairs for Beringer Blass Wine Estates (now Treasury Wine Estates), where she oversaw brand public relations for nearly two dozen wineries in California, Australia, Italy, New Zealand and Chile, and managed corporate affairs for the North American wine division of the Australian company, Fosters' Group. Prior to Beringer she worked at Ketchum Public Relations in its San Francisco and New York offices, where her accounts ranged from commodity boards to consumer packaged goods and insurance companies. Her interest in wine developed at Ketchum when she was assigned to the New York Wine & Grape Foundation to work on the "Uncork New York!" campaign. Cronin got her start in public relations at Edelman Public Relations in New York, following a two-year assignment in the publicity department of *Newsweek*.

Hanzell Vineyards Overcomes Problems with TCA Contamination

Michael Fineman

Situation and objective

Hanzell Vineyards is one of the original and most respected vintners in the Sonoma wine region of Northern California and among the most acclaimed producers of Pinot Noir and Chardonnay. In the summer of 2003, Hanzell Vineyards President Jean Arnold faced allegations from *Wine Spectator* Editor James Laube that Hanzell's wines were tainted by trichloroanisole (TCA), a health-harmless group of chemical compounds that can alter the taste of wine, from completely "corking" the wine in higher levels to subtly diminishing the wine's fruit in lower levels. In extremely low levels, some would argue up to three parts per trillion, it is undetectable with the exception of the most sophisticated wine consumer palates.

Hanzell was not the first wine to be taken to task by Laube for detected low levels of TCA. Laube is a voice for the wine consumer and his charges can be damaging. To make matters worse for the wineries criticized, their responses were rarely assuring. Seeking to clarify communication, Arnold engaged San Francisco-based Fineman PR to assist in crafting a response.

The primary objective was to assure the brand reputation manifested as deserving of trust and holding to high standards. That meant a forthright, responsible and informed response, a demonstrated commitment to wine consumers and the courage to treat the issue as an opportunity rather than a predicament.

The wine taint allegations were made by an editor of one of the world's best-read wine magazines, and the winery almost immediately began experiencing consumer and customer questions. Hanzell's challenge was compounded by the lack of established standards for acceptable TCA levels, with the sensory threshold for TCA awareness appearing to be a moving target.

Strategy

Arnold and Fineman put together an assertive communications campaign to demonstrate Hanzell's commitment to quality, good

112

faith and transparency. The winery had already been experiencing increasingly reduced market awareness due to the exposure of so many *new* wineries.

Arnold was determined to use this situation to rejuvenate the Hanzell image for a whole new generation of wine enthusiasts. She had a reputation in the wine business for marketing savvy, optimism, affability and progressiveness. *And Arnold knew how to rally*. The solution: assume marketplace leadership by addressing the issue responsibly and educating both the trade and concerned consumers about this little-known, wine product phenomenon.

Along the way, tell the Hanzell story, reinforce trade relationships and reach out to new audiences. The messages: Hanzell stands behind its wines, Hanzell stands for the best possible consumer experience, Hanzell continues to be a standard bearer for world class Pinot Noir and Chardonnay, and Hanzell is a leader in implementing new and better practices for the benefit of the marketplace.

Tactics and execution

In August 2003, Hanzell halted all sales and engaged a sensory analysis consultant who commissioned a focus group of wine-savvy consumers to sample and evaluate the wines for any possible sensory issues. That same month saw the release of a Hanzell-commissioned White Paper, authored by Master Sommelier Catherine Fallis, that discussed TCA, its origins, effects, its spread and its removal from winemaking environments. The sensory findings and White Paper were shared by Hanzell with customers, members of the trade and the media in regions throughout the country. In the best interests of the wine industry as a whole, Arnold even shared the information with other wineries, including market competitors.

Fineman PR released the results of the research and provided an update on the discoveries made about the source of the taint and the advancements Hanzell was making. Based on the sensory evaluations, the announcement reported the Chardonnay would be re-released (tasting results revealed no negative sensory discernments), and the Pinot Noir would be available to restaurants and retail purveyors only by request (its tasting proved less conclusive). In light of the *Wine Spectator* article that highlighted what the magazine believed was a problem, Fineman understood that a possible implication would be that Hanzell was in denial or that the winery was thumbing its nose at a powerful market influencer.

Arnold was confident in her wines and in her findings. From the highly positive marketplace feedback, Fineman recommended and organized a tasting of the wines for high-profile San Francisco wine writers and sommeliers at one of San Francisco's most prestigious restaurants. The 20+ wine professionals attending were invited to taste the wines in question and interview Arnold, Hanzell's sensory consultant and Fallis. The participants were impressed by the quality of the wine and its lack of discernable taint, the value of the information shared, Arnold's transparency, the winery's endeavor to act in good faith, and by Arnold's courage. The resulting media response was highly favorable.

Nine months later, a well-received open house was held to showcase the winery's rejuvenated facilities, including a new, state-of-the-art winery and barrel aging cave.

Evaluation of success

Media response was overwhelmingly affirmative, and the winery was hailed for its forthright, honest and knowledgeable approach to its potentially devastating challenge. The winery and its proud history were awarded new and enhanced recognition in the marketplace. As an added award for its openness and doing the right thing, many of the media contacts who'd shown an interest in the company's problems and its response covered the winery again in June 2004 when Hanzell celebrated its 50-year anniversary and unveiled its new facilities.

Results

Beginning with a cover story in the weekly wine section of *The San Francisco Chronicle,* the press reported on both the forthright way the company had discussed its challenge and solution, and the grace and leadership of Hanzell in sharing what it had learned at great expense. Among the acknowledgments from trade media was a *Wine Business Monthly* (12/03) article, "Hanzell Tells the Truth About TCA," and an in-depth *Vineyard and Winery Management* (1/04) piece, "Tackling TCA Contamination in the Cellar –Hanzell's Magnanimous Gift to the Wine Industry."

In the second phase of the PR program, in June 2004, several area newspapers sent reporters to tour and cover the new cave and winemaking facilities, resulting in a number of colorful feature stories with photos.

Return on investment

The positive feedback that Arnold received from customers and distributors and its subsequent positive publicity confirmed the winery's gain in new visibility, respect and rejuvenated sales, though it was by no means a slam dunk. "It's incredibly difficult to restart case sales after stopping for several months," says Arnold. "The sales people have a short memory, and it's tough to recapture their attention." As a capstone to Hanzell's public relations program, *Wine Spectator* also showed its respect, featuring Jean Arnold among women wine leaders less than two years after initiating Hanzell's crisis.

Arnold tells it like this. "Beginning in 1957, Hanzell helped pioneer the production of fine, estate-grown California Pinot Noir and Chardonnay and developed the style that wine lovers now associate with world class wines from Northern California. The wines were aged in French oak barrels, a rare practice then in California. The objective was to compete with the best wines that France had to offer and reflect the site-specific and distinctive terroir of these plantings. I felt a tremendous responsibility to carry on Hanzell's good name, its rich tradition and proud heritage.

Arnold says, "We went back to that research-based, pioneering tradition to get out in front of our challenge. We shared our learnings in consumer sensory thresholds, in winery sanitation protocols and in responding to criticism with truth and dignity. I was determined to show what our brand stands for…high standards in wine quality, integrity and in the credibility of our promise to consumers. A crisis like the one we faced gave us that opportunity, and we made the most of it in a demonstration *and communication* of good faith."

***

Michael Fineman, with more than 25 years of public relations, crisis communications and corporate consulting experience, formed Fineman PR in 1988 in San Francisco. Under his direction, the agency has built a national reputation for crisis communications, especially in the food and wine categories.

Fineman was named one of the PR profession's leading crisis communications counselors by PR Week. His high profile crisis experience includes campaigns for Foster Farms Poultry and issues related to Avian Influenza, animal rights activists and labor actions; food safety and product recalls for Odwalla, Fresh Express Farms, Foxy Produce and a host of other food companies; Pacifica Foundation's reopening of its embattled KPFA radio station in Berkeley, Calif.; institutions of higher education including Westmont College which battled rumors and accusations in the Santa Barbara Tea Fire, and for UC Santa Cruz when researchers' homes were bombed by animal rights terrorists; healthcare clients such as City of Hope Medical Group; and wine-related businesses for product quality allegations, environmental concerns and labor relations.

Fineman is a member of California's Wine Institute. His wine clients, both for marketing PR and issues management, have included Stag's Leap Wine Cellars, Chateau Montelena, King Estate, Hanzell Vineyards, Jackson Family Estates, Chalk Hill Vineyards, Derenoncourt California, Seguin Moreau, Moone-Tsai, Quivira, Landmark Vineyards and Arkenstone.

In his annual "Top 10 PR Blunders List," published in *USA Today, the Wall Street Journal* and *Time* magazine, Fineman advises corporations on what not to do during crisis situations by highlighting the year's most egregious public relations blunders.

Mumm: TV Answers "21 Bottle Salute"
Sam Folsom

Unlocking the secret to public relations success can be a frustrating pursuit, in large part because there is rarely a single answer. It's a combination of factors, some of which are within a publicist's control and some of which are not.

Tactical execution, writing skill, appropriate media contacts and the ability to recognize opportunities in a larger context all play an important role in the public relations process. And the underlying product, story and spokespeople factor heavily into the equation. Then there's creativity, which ranges from groundbreaking concepts to more nuanced tweaking of messages and tactics. A creative idea can breathe new life into an old story, and it can turn a mundane event into a must-see production.

Creativity in public relations need not involve a big concept to be effective, nor does it need to be expensive. Some of the most productive PR campaigns grow from more subtle ideas that add a creative flair rather than a big splash. The Mumm Napa harvest story provides a perfect example.

When Mumm Napa hired my firm, Folsom + Associates, one of their stated objectives was to generate more coverage of the start of harvest at the winery. As a sparkling wine house with vineyards in different regions of Napa Valley, they were usually the first winery in Napa to begin picking grapes. The start of harvest at Mumm Napa had been covered by the media, including television, in the past, but coverage had fallen off. The winery expressed interest in getting the press, particularly TV, back to the winery to cover the beginning of crush.

From a public relations standpoint, Mumm Napa had some important advantages. While the grape harvest starts earlier in warmer regions such as the Central Valley, Mumm Napa was the first to pick in Napa Valley, and Napa Valley had the name recognition and appeal with news media. Mumm Napa also had an established brand name, a reputation for quality and an affable winemaker who was comfortable in front of a camera. The public relations challenge was bringing the story to life for television.

We first developed the news angle with broader consumer appeal: The Napa Valley wine harvest was starting and it provided an ideal opportunity to talk about the wine business and the growing popularity of sparkling wine. Next we needed a visual component that would capture the attention of an assignment editor and make good TV. As a public relations tactic, we developed a concept we called the '21 Bottle Salute,' which would herald the first load of grapes to arrive at the winery. The '21 Bottle Salute' involved assembling the winery staff at the crushpad, arming each person with an unopened bottle of bubbly (vigorously shaken) and instructing the team to pop their corks on cue from the winemaker following his toast to the vintage. It provided a lively, colorful and festive backdrop to the arrival of the first grapes and a short talk by the winemaker on the start of harvest.

We pitched the news story on the start of harvest, along with a description of the winery's plans for a "21 Bottle Salute"'celebration, to TV assignment editors and producers in the San Francisco Bay Area. The combination of a news hook, a business story and a lively visual for TV proved very compelling as we generated feature story coverage on most of the major TV stations in the Bay Area.

To see the story on television, visit folsomandassociates.com.

***

Sam Folsom founded Folsom + Associates in San Francisco in 1993 and has built the agency into one of the leading firms in wine, food and lifestyle public relations. He is a veteran communications strategist with more than 20 years of experience in public relations and corporate communications. He has advised companies ranging from international corporations to up-and-coming boutique brands. His clients have included some of the world's leading wineries, restaurants and food companies.

Earlier in his career, Sam headed public relations and communications for Buena Vista/Racke USA and Louis M. Martini. He was previously media relations manager and industry spokesman for the Wine Institute. He began his career with Beringer Vineyards in the Napa Valley. He is a graduate of Vassar College. Reach him at sam@folsomandassociates.com.

History Comes to Life ...
Margie Healy

As a youngster, it's sad to say I had no interest in history. What I didn't stop to realize is that history is made everyday. It captures incredible stories, documents momentous events and gives us keen perspective on the present.

From my first day at Korbel in 1996, I realized that the Korbel story is more than a part of the history of winemaking in Sonoma County – it's the saga of two enterprising families with pioneer spirits and old-world resourcefulness who had a vision of what could be accomplished with the great opportunities emerging from the development of this country. Although generations apart, the Korbel and Heck families created and preserved a singular tradition of California champagne-making excellence that has now been in existence for 130 years. My job, as a public relations professional, is to sustain that tradition by keeping our brand "top of mind" – whether at a huge event or a small family gathering – anywhere memories are being made.

Flipping through the pages of Korbel's history, a trend emerges. Repeatedly, the winery has been chosen to celebrate historic milestones, including international sporting contests, political events and celebrity gatherings. Far back in 1933, Korbel began its long relationship with American politics, by shipping a case of Korbel Sec to President Franklin D. Roosevelt to toast the repeal of Prohibition. Korbel was prominently served at numerous state dinners and presidential events by John and Jackie Kennedy during the Camelot years of the White House. In 1985, Korbel was chosen to be served at the Inauguration of Ronald Reagan and has continued this tradition through the Inaugurations of George H. W. Bush in 1989, Bill Clinton in 1993 and 1998, George W. Bush in 2001 and 2005, and Barack Obama in 2009.

It goes without saying that such a historic celebration deserves to be toasted with American champagne, especially one with deep roots in our country's most memorable occasions such as Korbel. But this honor does not automatically happen. Every four years Korbel is asked to make a presentation to the Joint Congressional Committee on Inaugural Ceremonies (JCCIC). Once approved,

Korbel winemakers create a unique commemorative Inaugural Cuvée of its Korbel Natural California Champagne to be served and raised in toasts to the administration at the Inaugural Luncheon following the swearing-in ceremonies. This is surely a prestigious honor that Korbel is extremely proud of and certainly never takes for granted.

In 2005, as I had done for the past three Inaugurations, I had the opportunity to work on this project with one huge difference – this time I was invited to attend the various inaugural events to include the actual Inauguration on the National Mall. To say I was honored and excited was an understatement. In public relations we have a tendency to elaborate the details, but when I say I still get chills thinking about the event, I am not exaggerating!

The buzz in Washington during inaugural week was unlike any I had witnessed on my past trips to the capital. Dressing up in evening wear to attend the pre-inaugural events was thrilling. Mixing with the Beltway VIPs was so interesting and enlightening. Then, when I picked up my ticket, I noticed that my seat for the Inauguration was marked "Platform". Nothing could have prepared me for this! I would actually be sitting with the entire Inaugural party in the most coveted seats of all.

On January 20, 2005, I arrived at the Capitol quite early so I could absorb everything leading up to the big event. I handed my ticket to an officer from the Marine Corps who escorted me to the platform and asked for my name. I immediately thought I was in the wrong place! But no – quite amazingly – his name was Healy, too! My seat was ten rows from the podium where George W. Bush would recite the oath of office. As I sat there among the gradually-filling seats looking down at the monuments, I couldn't believe how fortunate I was to be there.

As the seats filled, history came to life. The who's who of American politics walked right in front of me including Presidents Carter, Bush and Clinton as well as George W. and Laura Bush. The platform hushed as ailing Chief Justice William Rehnquist processed in with other members of the Supreme Court. NBC's Andrea Mitchell was interviewing people right below my seat. Interestingly, I recall her interviewing a young, somewhat unknown senator from Illinois – Barack Obama. As the morning progressed and the patriotic music played on, I felt so proud to be an American.

After President Bush took his oath of office and delivered his Inaugural address, he was escorted to Statuary Hall in the U.S. Capitol for the traditional Inaugural Luncheon. Since 1897, the Inaugural Luncheon has been one of the most exclusive events of the Presidential Inauguration. In addition to the President, Vice President and members of their families, the 200 invited guests included the senior members of the Senate and House of Representatives, Supreme Court Justices, members of the President's Cabinet, former Presidents and me, Margie Healy!

As I walked away from the Capitol that blustery afternoon, I wasn't cold at all – rather I was filled with the warm memories of the awe-inspiring spectacle I just experienced.

Working on this iconic brand has been such an incredible education and has afforded me opportunities that I never could have envisioned. But this day certainly was the highlight of my career. To promote Korbel, we have used the tagline – *Korbel turns moments into memories* - and having witnessed an unforgettable moment in history, I couldn't agree more!

***

Margie Healy, a 36-year veteran of the California wine industry, joined Korbel as Director of Public Relations in 1996. Before joining Korbel, she was Director of Winery Member Relations at the Wine Institute and held a public relations position at Browne Vintners. She has held several board positions with Wine Institute, Women for WineSense, the American Institute of Wine and Food and others. Her email address is mhealy@korbel.com.

Sutter Home's Build-a-Better-Burger Contest
Stan Hock

During the mid-1980s, profound changes began occurring in the American wine business. Previously, wine in the U.S. was sold primarily in restaurants, wine shops and liquor stores, and generic "jug" wines dominated the market. However, as affluent, well-traveled baby boomers began embracing wine as their alcoholic beverage of choice and trading up from jug wines to premium varietals, supermarket executives saw the profit potential in offering their customers a broad selection of high-quality wines. Within a few years, large grocery chains like Safeway, Kroger and Publix dramatically enlarged and upgraded their wine inventories, and a major new venue for wine suppliers emerged.

There remained a problem. Surveys indicated that only ten percent of grocery shoppers passed through their store's wine section. If wineries were to take full advantage of supermarket sales opportunities, they needed to break out of the wine section and gain displays of their products in the meat, produce, frozen food and deli departments.

But the managers of those departments, charged with maximizing the profitability of shelf and floor display space, jealously guarded their real estate. If a steak sauce display regularly generated a healthy profit for the meat department manager, why would he or she turn over its space to an unproven product like wine?

The key, decided Sutter Home Winery, an early innovator in wine marketing, was to persuade store managers that displaying wine would help them sell more meat, cheese, fish, condiments, paper goods, etc. To do so, Sutter Home's marketers devised colorful displays, case cards, shelf talkers and bottle neckers depicting Sutter Home wines accompanying appetizing meals featuring everyday grocery items.

Although this effort was aimed primarily at selling more Sutter Home wine, it had an ancillary benefit. What little marketing wineries had done to that point, whether in advertising or via point-of-sale merchandising, typically portrayed wine with fancy foods like poached salmon or filet mignon, reinforcing most Americans' perception that wine was a beverage for the elite.

Sutter Home, a fast-growing producer of popularly priced premium wines (*i.e.*, $4-$6 per bottle), had a vested interest in persuading consumers that wine could be enjoyed on a daily basis with everyday foods like chicken, spaghetti, pizza and hamburgers. By associating its wines with the food preferences of average Americans, Sutter Home positioned itself as the "consumer-friendly" winery.

Building A Better Burger

Searching for a way to drive home its wine-for-everyday theme in dramatic, mass-merchandisable fashion, Sutter Home, in 1990, created what was to become a landmark wine industry promotion: the Build a Better Burger (BBB) recipe contest. A national competition offering a $10,000 Grand Prize (since raised to $20,000), the contest is open to any backyard chef with the imagination to concoct a creative, appetizing burger. Any ingredients are permissible, provided they can be formed into a patty and fit into a bun or other bread product. Over the years, entries have run the gamut from southwestern trout burgers and vegetarian black bean burgers to mu shu pork burgers and beyond.

The winery bolstered the appeal of the promotion to the grocery trade by partnering with major food companies like Kraft and Del Monte, which participated in the first BBB promotion by offering discount coupons on an assortment of grilling-related products. Since then, co-sponsors have included the Beef Council, Tabasco, the California Avocado Commission and the United States Potato Board, among others. This co-partnering and cross merchandising among wine and food companies and commodity boards subsequently became *de rigeur* for other large wineries like Gallo, Glen Ellen, Fetzer and Mondavi, and continues unabated today.

To invest Build a Better Burger with credibility in the food world, Sutter Home hired James McNair, a best-selling cookbook author and Napa Valley resident, to be head judge of the contest. Each year, McNair assembles a distinguished panel of well-known chefs, cookbook authors and food writers to judge the finalists' recipes (previously selected by McNair from thousands of entries) at a Grand Prize cook-off held in late September at Sutter Home. At the event, a festive affair now open to the public, the finalists prepare their burgers for the judges, who select the cash prize winners based on originality, taste appeal and ease of preparation.

From the beginning, Build a Better Burger has generated widespread media coverage for Sutter Home. Each May the winery sends a wire press release announcing the contest to 2,000 food writers throughout the U.S. (BBB runs from Memorial Day through Labor Day, ensuring that colorful Build a Better Burger displays remain in stores throughout the summer.) In recent years, the winery has also distributed a fully formatted matte release containing fun facts about burgers that finds its way into hundreds of newspaper food columns, as well as numerous cooking contest newsletters.

Sutter Home also places BBB advertising inserts in the summer grilling issues of leading national food magazines, further extending the contest's exposure. "Building a Better Burger" stories are now commonplace in such magazines. In addition, the winery's heavily trafficked website aggressively promotes the contest, providing consumers with downloadable contest entry forms and previous years' prizewinning recipes.

BBB has also penetrated book and broadcast media. In 1992, San Francisco's Chronicle Books published *James McNair's Burgers*, a cookbook inspired by the contest, which in turn spawned The *Sutter Home Wine Country Cookbook*, also published by Chronicle. On the broadcast media side, Sutter Home has sent its talented in-house chef, Jeffrey Starr, around the country to promote the contest by demonstrating the art of building better burgers on local and national TV cooking shows. BBB has been featured in a PBS series on America's leading cooking contests and on a Food Network program showcasing northern California's food scene. And for the past five years, the contest cook-off has been broadcast live on KGO Radio, San Francisco's ABC affiliate, by nationally syndicated personality Gene Burns, a well-known gourmet whose show reaches millions of listeners.

Finally, by inviting leading food media to attend the cook-off and disseminating a post-event press release announcing the contest's Grand Prize winner, the winery generates further media coverage and stimulates consumer interest in the following year's contest.

The Build a Better Burger franchise has helped Sutter Home extend its brand identity as the premium winery that takes the pretense out of wine and makes it fun and accessible to the "average" consumer. Promoting the idea that wine enhances the humblest of meals and provides everyday pleasure has become commonplace in winery advertising and public relations.

Images of snooty aesthetes haughtily fingering tastevins are now relics of yesteryear. Today, in TV ads, billboards and store displays, consumers see people like themselves drinking unpretentious wines with pasta, Chinese food and America's favorite sandwich, the burger.

***

Stanley Hock is a public relations consultant. Before establishing his own business, he served for 13 years as director of communications at Trinchero Family Estates/ Sutter Home Winery in Napa Valley.

During his 25-year career in the wine business, Hock has also been a fine wine retailer and a widely published wine writer. He collaborated with James McNair on the *Sutter Home Napa Valley Cookbook*, published by Chronicle Books, and is co-author of *Harvesting the Dream: The Rags-To-Riches Tale of the Sutter Home Winery*, published by John Wiley & Sons.

Hock lives in Kensington, Calif. and can be reached at zinfanatic@aol.com.

Copia Faces the "Pooping Pope" Crisis
Kathleen Iudice

It wasn't enough that Copia: The American Center for Wine, Food & the Arts in Napa opened just after September 11, 2001, and in the midst of a severe economic downturn. It soon faced a public relations nightmare that eventually proved a bonanza, so much so that the innovative new interactive museum was wrongly accused of staging a sneaky PR coup by initiating the controversy.

The catalyst for the incident was some tiny figurines in an artwork about world hunger.

The piece by Catalonian artist Antoni Miralda consisted of a number of display cases that illustrated all aspects of world hunger, from starvation to excess and everything in between. It also showed recycling.

Among the found objects, Miralda incorporated some tiny squatting figurines called "caganers." Caganers are an old Catalonia tradition—one of recycling/rebirth, and are secreted in nativity scenes where they are thought to bring good luck to the children who find them.

In the old days, they were of shepherds or other rural figures, but now they include topical representations, including political figures and, in this case, a nun and a bishop –but not the Pope, as was incorrectly alleged by the local alternative weekly newspaper, *Napa Sentinel.*

Of course Catalonians, and Europeans in general, are less prudish than many Americans, and some people here took exception to the objects. Unfortunately, the publisher of the *Sentinel*, who also sat on the City Council at the time, was confused and highly offended by the objects. He wrote about a 'pooping Pope statue,' and sent copies to the extremist Catholic League political action group (basically two men who flood supporters with e-mails). They, in turn, urged people to complain to Copia, which they did with abundant zeal.

"We were bombarded with irate calls, many obscene, as well as hundreds of e-mails about the 'pooping Pope statue'," says Kathleen Iudice, former public relations manager at Copia.

"At first, we didn't even know what they were talking about and had to search the exhibit," she says. "When we discovered the 'culprit,' we were amused and issued a statement (below) thinking that would be the end of it. But they wouldn't acknowledge it - as if the truth just got in the way."

Fortunately, *Associated Press* in Barcelona heard about the controversy and distributed a piece on the caganers. Soon the tide turned.

People started to write letters of support, and many publications and broadcast media covered the controversy, almost all positively. The local *Napa Valley Register* supported Copia throughout the debacle with features, commentaries and daily postings of pro/con "Letters to the Editor."

The center benefited from a trial-in-crisis communications, which was incorporated into the development of a crisis communications plan that included:

- Give people more information to start with.
- Be forthright and consistent. The truth will speak for itself.
- Always take the high ground.

"The whole process allowed us to restate Copia's commitment to artistic freedom," says Iudice. "Ironically, the attention it generated for Copia resulted in more people visiting."

It also created a great deal of work for Iudice and her staff —who continued to receive media inquires about the issue throughout Copia's existence. Unfortunately, the organization closed in 2008.

Response to letters and e-mails

Iudice prepared the following response for the letters, e-mails and phone calls:

Thank you for sharing your concerns with us regarding the Catholic League's current campaign.

Regrettably, their news release was sent out with misinformation about elements of an artwork, "Collections/Selections: Food

Culture Museum," within the main exhibition, "Active Ingredients," that they have never seen.

The element that they are referencing as "the work of Antoni Miralda" is a tiny component within Miralda's artwork, which is comprised of 11 soda-machines filled with worldly food-related "found" objects. The figurines, each no larger than a chess piece, were purchased by the artist at a Christmas fair in Barcelona and are part of a group of 35 comical figurines that occupy just three out of six shelves in one of the 11 exhibit cases.

The figurines are "caganers," a Catholic Catalan folk art tradition originating in Barcelona, Spain (Miralda's home), and date back to the 18th century. Caganers are traditionally included in Catalan nativity scenes for comic effect, and to ensure luck, health, peace and tranquility of spirit throughout the coming year. To have these figures absent is thought to bring misfortune.

Please note that the Catholic League also included incorrect budget information. Copia did not receive $70 million in funds from the State of California, nor did it receive taxpayer's money from the City of Napa. In fact, Copia spent over one million dollars for city improvements as part of its agreement to build in Napa.

***

Kathleen Iudice has over 20 years experience in marketing/branding, public relations, hospitality and sales, with an emphasis on wine, food, tourism, community and the arts. Her work experience includes marketing manager for Far Niente Winery, marketing/sales director for Stonegate Winery, national marketing/sales director for Niebaum-Coppola Estate Winery, marketing/PR advisor for Old Sacramento, and marketing/project director for The B Street Theatre and the Sacramento Ballet. As the public relations manager for Copia: The American Center for Wine, Food & the Arts, she managed the communications and helped develop promotions for a multitude of programs and activities, including gardens, exhibitions, performing arts, special events, and the on-premise retail store and restaurants.

Most recently, she has worked with the City of Winters on their branding/marketing campaign, Simi Winery's Fall Forage event, the Napa Fresh Aire Festival, the launch of Neela's in Napa, the launch of the Farm Bureau's Tractor Festival, the launch of Marketta Winery and Vineyards, Napa Downtown Association's Press Tout, and Preservation Napa Valley's annual Barn Tour; and she continues to work with Howie's Artisan Pizza in Palo Alto, PR for the annual Napa Truffle Festival, and Red Barn Studios workshops in Granite Bay.

She studied art at the Academy of Art University, has a degree in Humanities from SFSU and is a Bauman Certified Nutrition Educator.

Wine Public Relations Today
by Julie Ann Kodmur

Ten years ago I was honored to contribute a chapter to *Spinning The Bottle*. I enjoyed assembling some very specific challenges and solutions for assorted winery priorities and programs. Fast forward: today the earth has moved under our feet. The paradigm has not only shifted but cracked and splintered. So this time, rather than offering specific challenges and solutions, I'll get both philosophical and tactical. Here goes.

A splintered paradigm? What do I mean? In the olden days the roles were very clear: you are a winery; I am the publicist; somewhere out there are very distinct groups we're trying to reach——differentiated members of the trade as well as The Consumer. Today those roles are blurred; everyone is a consumer and to some degree everyone is a journalist. This makes publicizing a wine a different kind of challenge than it ever used to be. Your message has to ring true whether the person listening is a wine buff sitting at home in Miami or the winery's distributor in Dubuque or a retailer in Redondo Beach or a restaurateur in Chicago. You can't have a different message any more for the different tiers; on top of that, your marketing and publicity efforts are transparent to the world, in a way new to our culture and business practices.

Here's another way to look at this: everyone is a member of the media today; any one can start a blog, broadcast their opinion and get a buzz going. Any one can go on an online bulletin board and begin a new thread, attract followers and have an impact, whether positive or negative.

What does that mean in terms of publicity tactics to implement? It means that the enlightened winery client should direct their publicist to work on a healthy mix of coverage – scores from the main wine periodicals *as well as* lengthy feature profiles in newspapers and magazines, nice scores and/or memorable narrative from wine bloggers, discussion on the online chat boards with some radio and television sprinkled in as well. Get the winemaker or proprietor out on the road, mingling in the real world, at stores and restaurants and wine events. Be visible; go broad; start building your stories. And don't forget to be real.

The publicist also needs to go deep and present lots of stories about the winery. Write them up. Put them up on the winery's website, with high-resolution downloadable photographs nearby. Give people lots of options and ideas. Make them feel they've discovered something about ABC Winery, an angle they can pursue and make their own. Remember that people are always Googling around and that often a visitor will arrive on the winery's website not through the "front door," the home page.

Books have been written about the importance of websites – and of course today, blogs and Facebook pages are that much more important in terms of the public face of a winery. So that brings us to language: if the tenor and tone of the verbiage on a website are appealing enough, friendly but not condescending, provocative but not negative, etc., you will find you're inspiring the reader to want to write about your winery.

Imagine being able to hand your winery's press kit to thousands of people at the same time: that's what the website really does. One example in my world was waking up one morning to find a post by 1WineDude (aka Joe Roberts), riffing not only on a client's Chardonnay but also on the winery's name, downloading one photo from the website and also going to the trouble to search for a very specific companion image to complete his coverage. Here it is, from December 2009: you can tell just from this excerpt that he enjoyed the vibe of the winery's website: "Not only was the Smith-Madrone a welcome departure from the often (too) heavily-oaked Chardonnay being made along Highway 29, it's also fairly priced at $30 (another nice departure from the usual Highway 29 fare). There's tropical fruit, but also a broad spectrum of stone-related flavors and aromas (pear, minerals), all in a nuanced and elegant taste presentation. One thing I wondered after visiting smithmadrone.com: are the Smiths ever worried about copyright infringement lawsuits from Smith Brothers? I mean, the names and the beards. I'm not sure I'd buy that it was a coincidence."

www.1winedude.com/index.php/2009/12/14/of-spouses-samples-and-92-point-flawed-wines/

Back to that newly shifted paradigm and how to execute against it.

Take advantage of another trend – the new (in relative terms) hyper-local outlets, whether it's the Patch franchise across the country or efforts such as *The New York Times*' Bay Citizen in the San Francisco Bay area. Communicate "smaller" news from the winery to the local paper; it might be something like a wine club activity or even new releases. That first outreach or two or three might not get covered, but ultimately your target on the local level will use something you provide, or contact you with other ideas. And when something does run, guess what? It's no longer little or local, it's up on the web, searchable, findable, another way of fleshing out the winery's personality and differentiating characteristics.

Not so new but taking new shape is the need to listen. Today more than ever a publicist has no excuse not to be tracking coverage and monitoring a winery's image, primarily as manifested online. Most publicists start their day reviewing Google alerts as well as who was tweeting about what to whom.

Look at the new Storify, which aggregates chatter on the web by subject matter – "real-time curation," as founders Burt Herman and Xavier Damman call it. You can't just forcefeed your winery's story any more; you need to see how it's being discussed, what kind of stories are showing up. You might discover a complaint on an online bulletin board and insert yourself in the mix to clean that up. That then will generate further chatter, ideally all to the good, about how responsive the winery is. That just happened to me, where I responded to a Canadian consumer on CellarTracker on behalf of a client, and saw the complimentary comments cascade in. The bottom line here is constant vigilance, the crucial importance to monitor essentially 24/7. And as we all have seen, the web is also in some ways the re-creation of the Wild West, where unfortunately nastiness and negativity can show up as frequently as positive and enthusiastic comments and chatter.

In my chapter in the first *Spinning The Bottle*, I shared the success of The Zin Zone, the "green room" for media at the annual Zinfandel Advocates & Producers' Festival in San Francisco. It's worth mentioning again, since making life easier for journalists never gets old or irrelevant. This past year one blogger even panned the room and put that video up on his blog, since The

Zin Zone has taken on a life of its own as a place where the media feel catered to: The Zin Zone has also always served another function which the journalists welcome: it's a way to make a large wine event smaller and digestible, more intimate and welcoming.

More recently, again looking to personalize what looks like a wine event too overwhelming to absorb, ZAP offered Zin Trails, a different way to look at finding wineries at the Festival, using helpful and logical variables as well as fun and unexpected variables. That meant that not only could you travel through the tasting looking for wineries by appellation, by price points, whether they farm organically, whether they have old vine vineyards, whether they offer single vineyard Zinfandels, whether they have women winemakers, whether they're first, second, third, fourth, fifth or sixth generation vintners, whether they make Zinfandel blends and—the variable which was most discussed – the winemaker's hair color! Who knew that could range from "gorgeous gray" to "silver fox" to "is bald a color" and "what hair" to "purple during harvest" to "blackberry?"

Another idea: it's human nature to enjoy conflict, protagonists and antagonists, a lively story with "heroes" and "villains." In the aftermath of *Sideways*, I worked with a winery to excite the trade about the merits of Merlot, building a program both online and in the real world called MerlotFightsBack, complete with a subtle graphic background of boxing gloves on a comment page on the site. Lots of traffic, lots of chatter; everyone loves an underdog!

Ten years later, what does it all boil down to? Don't forget old-fashioned boots-on-the- ground publicity practices: make sure you have well-written materials and lots of person to person contact. Never stop thinking "what if!" Have fun – there's an idea (or a blogger) waiting under every tree!

***

Julie Ann Kodmur is a publicity and marketing consultant and freelance journalist. She received her B.A. from Stanford University and did master's degree course work at NYU's Institute of Fine Arts. She has been a panelist on publicity and marketing topics at numerous wine industry symposia and in

1997 founded her own marketing and publicity consultancy. She lives in St. Helena with her family and speaks fluent Italian and conversational French and German. Contact her at www.julieannkodmur.com or (707) 963-9632.

Done In by a Dachshund
Keith Love

We are fortunate at Stimson Lane that there have been many PR successes for Chateau St. Michelle, Columbia Crest, Conn Creek and our other wineries.

But what you always remember are the failures.

Here is my biggest failure.

In 2000 Chateau Ste. Michelle completed a huge new barrel room on the historic Chateau grounds near Seattle.

All of our grapes are grown east of the Cascades, where there are 17 hours of sunlight each day through the summer, and where the desert-steppe nights provide a chill that contributes to the acidity and crispness for balance.

By 2000 we had run out of barrel space at the Chateau. So the new barrel facility for our Chardonnays and Sauvignon Blancs was eagerly awaited.

Our president, Ted Baseler, wandered into my office at the Chateau and said he sure hoped we would be able to get some Seattle TV for the official opening of our grand barrel facility.

I told him we'd do our best, but I reminded him that local TV news in Seattle—as in most places—had evolved into hysterical crime reports that sometimes bordered on the absurd—even purse snatchings could get top billing.

I wasn't so sure the opening of a barrel room for the state's oldest and most prestigious winery would capture the fancy of assignment editors at the TV stations in Seattle.

However, I managed to get a commitment from the producer for Seattle's highest rated station. (I won't mention the name because, well, I still may need them!)

The producer said, "Keith, we have one satellite truck with time on Thursday at 2 p.m. Here is what I need from you. I need for your president to be ready to go on camera for a standup. I need a cooper there, and he needs to be French and to speak with a French accent. And he needs to be wearing a beret."

I used to cover national politics for the *Los Angeles Times*, so I was familiar with the "priorities" of TV producers. Fine.

I took my challenge to our white-wine maker and he said, "No problem. As it happens, Seguin Moreau has a cooper from Europe visiting at their Napa offices and I will have him come up. I will even tell him he has to wear a beret."

Thursday morning arrived and Erik alerted me that the cooper was on the grounds and is setting up his toasting flame and the staves and rings so that he coul make several barrels on the lawn near the new barrel room.

I called the TV producer and he said, "Yep, you are still on the schedule. But, as you know, Keith, if big news breaks, we will have to stiff you. That's the breaks."

At around 1 p.m. I wandered down to meet the cooper and make sure he would be ready.

What a nasty surprise. This is the kind of thing that keeps PR people up all night.

The cooper was not a Frenchman. He was a Scot. He was not wearing a beret. He had on a kilt.

And he had the thickest Scottish brogue since Sean Connery made James Bond movies.

I threw a fit when I finally found the winemaker. He apologized with a Gallic shrug. But there was nothing he could do about it.

Suddenly, my cell phone rang. It was the TV producer. He said, "Man, I hate to do this to you, but the satellite truck has been pulled off for a breaking story that is going on right now at a motel complex near downtown Seattle."

Whew! Obviously, given the screw-up with the cooper, I was relieved the TV crew was not coming. The producer and his on-air reporter would not have been happy to see a Scotsman in a kilt rather than a Frenchman in a beret.

But I pretended to be profoundly disappointed as I responded to the producer. He said, "I'm sorry, I'm sorry, I'm sorry. I owe you one."

He added, "You might want to watch the first newscast tonight at 5. The story on the motel will be the lead-in."

At 5 p.m I turned on the TV in my office. Sure enough, there was the motel story. Imagine my reaction when I saw what had taken my satellite truck.

A tourist from Kansas had lost her dachshund after checking into the motel. The dog had somehow gotten into the heating and air conditioning system at the motel. They could hear its lonely cries deep in the duct system of the motel. The owner was sobbing on camera. Fire trucks were lined up and the firemen were trying to locate the dog using the motel's duct system schematic.

If you have ever watched local TV news anywhere in America, you know I am not making this up.

Our 18,000 new French oak barrels missed their 15 minutes of fame but I was smiling.

***

Keith Love was Vice President of Communications for Ste. Michelle Wine Estates (formerly Stimson Lane) from 1999 until he retired in 2009. Keith's career has included stints at *The New York Times* and the *Los Angeles Times*. He was also press secretary for Washington Gov. Gary Locke.

Charles Shaw and its PR Lessons

Harvey Posert

Charles "Two-buck Chuck" Shaw wines have been a phenomenal sales success, and media —with public relations work —has played an important role. With no marketing campaign by Bronco Wine Co., the producer, nor by Trader Joe's, the sole retailer, you still have probably heard about the wine from seven network news programs, AP, Reuters, the *Los Angeles Times* or a hundred other sources. But in the beginning it was word-of-mouth.

The Charles Shaw phenomenon demonstrates some basic ideas about public relations —concepts relating to the public's interests—and publicity, skill in handling media.

First, be an early, clear example of a trend. These days, good wine does not have to be expensive. We're making good wine all over California and many places overseas. Media have jumped on the negative news of the glut.

Second, take a leadership position. The Franzia family at Bronco has been successful at grapegrowing, producing, distributing and marketing, building brands known for quality and value. Before Charles Shaw, there were Forest Glen, Montpellier, Hacienda, Forestville and a dozen other brands.

Third, make a dramatic statement. As bulk wine prices fell, an efficient wine operation like Bronco could work with a niche retailer like Trader Joe's to market good wine profitably at $1.99.

Fourth, look for a positive industry slant to the story. At that price, wine is being bought by the occasional wine buyer and served to the very occasional wine drinker, helping to bring in new consumers to an industry which spends embarrassingly little to increase consumption.

Is there a pro bono angle? As near as we can tell, Charles Shaw first became visible when an *Los Angeles Times* executive kept seeing it at charity functions; it has become known as the "fundraisers' wine" there. The first feature story, by the *Times'* Corie Brown, was so well done that it was reprinted all over the country.

Actually, *Wines & Vines* had the story first, printing a short item ("Wine Notes," Sept.. 2002) on a staff tasting where Shaw was preferred over a $67 Chardonnay.

We were able to use the magazine as an authority to document quality and value.

Bring the writer into the story. Not hard, when it seemed that every media person had read about it, heard about it or tasted it. Remember that journalists are trained to be suspicious and objective. Yet I still sensed that basically writers who write about wine identify with our products, as they have during the 38 years I've been involved. And in California, if the region makes wine, chances are there's a local grape involved.

The wine had been out about a year. Word-of-mouth had been building in Southern California during 2002, and as the holiday season approached, people moved from buying bottles to cases. Apparently, this is the modus operandi of the Trader Joe's consumer. He buys a little, brings it home and tastes it, and if he likes it he returns to buy a lot. He's afraid it may not be there in a month, but in the case of Charles Shaw, it was.

So the *L.A. Times'* December story was the "tipping point." At my son. Bob's, Irvine, Calif. office, the company reprinted the story for all employees and put it in the lunchroom. Although Trader Joe's didn't get involved, the story moved to other print and broadcast wine lovers.

Media love the counter-cyclical story, a success in a down period or vice versa.

With an estimated 10,000-plus labels fighting over a static market, only this one moved from marketing "push" to "pull." Conventional publicity rules applied: have the facts, respond immediately and look for some supporting authorities.

You want to build the writer's confidence and expertise. In addition to *Wines & Vines,* industry analyst Jon Fredrikson was enormously helpful in making some estimates and putting the story in an industry context.

Since Bronco executives seldom talk to the press, the story was gleaned mostly from consumers, adding to the third-party endorsement that makes publicity so valuable. And some of the best consumer responses were on wine chat rooms.

We used their reviews and responses with media, showing that although some gave the wine scores in the 70s, most were in the 80s, and no one could argue with the value. A couple of bad reviews, in fact, gave the material believability, not your everyday PR action!

And it was a Trader Joe's employee on a chat room who gave Charles Shaw the nickname that media loved, "Two-buck Chuck!"

In the nine years since Charles Shaw's introduction at Trader Joe's, there have been over 600,000,000 bottles sold. The wine and its nickname have truly become part of the language, often signifying a product which is both quality and inexpensive. Songs, clothing and other products are using the names. There is a Facebook page which neither Bronco Wine Company nor Trader Joe's handle, and many daily mentions — too many!

Now with the tenth anniversary at some point in 2012, we're discussing an appropriate commemorative bottle: Charles Shaw Sparkling Wine? Charles Shaw Import Selections? Two-Buck Chuck Reserve? Wait and see.

***

Harvey Posert is a former newspaperman who managed the Wine Institute account for international PR firm Edelman from 1965-1975, then served as WI's public relations director until 1980, when he took a similar position at Robert Mondavi. In 2004 he received Advertising Age's Marketing 50 Award. He is now a PR consultant. See www.harveyposert.com.

Creating a Niche for an Unknown Variety
Peter Posert

In 1995 I became sales and marketing director at Chateau Benoit Winery in Oregon. Like most Oregon wineries, they produced Pinot Noir, Pinot Gris, Chardonnay and White Riesling, but their mainstay was a little known variety called Müller-Thurgau, which makes a pretty, semi-sweet white wine. It accounted for more than half of the winery's production at the time and was the most consistent wine the winery produced. Chateau Benoit Winery was by far the largest producer of the variety in North America. Yet few people knew much about Müller-Thurgau.

Almost all of the wine was sold for low prices in Oregon in local groceries, tasting rooms or as a summer wine. Morale among the other producers was low, since the price was low. The state was losing acreage, as vines were getting replaced by other varieties or just ripped out. The local high-end Pinot Noir producers scoffed at the wine with regularity and ridicule. This led to an inferiority complex amongst the various producers, many of who ridiculed the variety themselves (while they were trying to sell it!).

Those few people that actually knew much about Müller-Thurgau understood that it makes the plonk whites of Germany, producing Liebfraumilch and Blue Nun.

The one main positive thing about Müller-Thurgau that I found is that almost everyone likes the flavor. The best times to drink the wine is with anything hot, be it a summer day or spicy foods. With the high natural acidity, lower alcohol and lightly sweet finish, the wine was made for the American palate the way a cool soda or a lightly sweet iced drink works. Most people recognized Müller-Thurgau's place if put in the right perspective. In reality, Müller-Thurgau is just plain fun.

In analyzing the situation, I realized I had a fantastic opportunity –the kind that rarely happens to wine salesmen. I had the chance to create a new variety in America!

I applied a few basic truisms about the wine business:

- For every wine variety successful in a region, industry pundits and gatekeepers will recognize one person (at least) as the authority about that wine.
- The perception that smaller production makes better wine than larger production.
- Wine writers and media are looking for new stories.
- Food associations give credence to wine.
- Anti-snobbery is acceptable. Most people don't like wine snobs.

With Oregon Müller-Thurgau, I made a few strategic decisions that allowed the variety to become successfully marketed in over 25 states within four years while raising prices and production levels.

I began by organizing a meeting of all the 16 producers of the variety in Oregon. I used the local wine trade association, the Oregon Wine Advisory Board, as the catalyst for the meeting, giving credence to the project at the outset.

The team's goal at the outset was to *raise consumer awareness*. My goal was also to create a working team that could be proud of the wine. I also thought that any other producer's promotions regarding Muller-Thurgau would come back to me as the main expert if I took a leadership role as the spokesperson for the largest producer.

I feel that the larger producers of every variety (whether there is 5 cases or 5 million cases) have a responsibility to do industry-wide marketing due to their role as the flagship of that variety.

We decided to: a) create a marketing brochure describing the wine; b) have a seminar at an upcoming meeting of the Society of Wine Educators, and c) send wine *together* to create an Oregon Müller-Thurgau category.

Our first big break was having one of the producers, Trudy Kramer of Kramer Vineyards, serve on the Oregon Wine Advisory Board (OWAB).

She knew about a little-used item in the Board's budget called "The Varietal Matching Grant Program." Basically, the state matched us dollar-for-dollar for any approved project, cutting the costs in half.

We needed a hook line so we coined the phrase "Heat Needs Sweet." It was repeated many times in sales calls, sales staff meetings and later with media people, so it became a mantra. That phrase sold more wine and developed more believers than almost anything.

Creating The Brochure

We received grants for basic research, writing and producing the brochure. At the OWAB grant meeting, one of the board members stated, "no state money should go to such a worthless variety as Müller-Thurgau as it would reflect so poorly on the wine community!" This was not unexpected. Yet we overcame that issue by noting that there were taxes paid from Müller-Thurgau production.

At the same time, we turned to the local wine research university, Oregon State University in Corvallis, for research information. We unexpectedly got our second big break. One of the OSU viticulture professors had studied at Geisenheim, Germany and Wadenswil, Switzerland, the two European wine schools that have competed for a century as the home of the variety. The professor knew everything there was to know about the variety, had done extensive research herself about the cross, had photos and a slide show of the mother vineyard and Dr. Muller-Thurgau, and had a wealth of information and stories that made our research easy and professional.

The Society of Wine Educators

The Society of Wine Educators forum attracted over 50 educators to hear about the new variety. Learning about a new domestic variety was a natural step for them to take. For our team, it allowed us to successfully work together one more time and get more gatekeepers on the team.

The critical journals

For the first year or two, we all sent our wine in to the various critical magazines together. What happened was sort of funny. Everyone got scores between 83 and 88. Nobody got a 90. Nobody was in the 70's. We all had pretty good wine, which is about what we thought we had before the project started. We did get our own category though.

Outcome

As the program evolved, each winery was accumulating a file of information to become better marketers. Self-doubt and local ridicule had been slowed or stopped. Producers were starting to feel better about themselves and their wines, less bashful about showing them internationally and around the country. Prices started to rise and inventories started to shrink. After just three years of work, the planted acreage of Muller-Thurgau started to rise in Oregon again, as people saw a future for the variety.

Slowly the writers started to see something and the stories began. By the end of my time at Chateau Benoit, we were getting stories about every three months. The wine was featured on television, radio and many times in print around the country.

Ultimately, the other wineries referred the inquiring writer to me (since I started the project and housed all the basic material and research) and we kept the stories coming by referring back to the other wineries as well, to make sure that everyone got their due.

In many respects, being the main advocate for a variety of pretty good wine was a fantastic opportunity. Inclusiveness, dedication, a jovial attitude and hard work were the common traits among the Muller-Thurgau working group.

***

Peter Posert is a negociant of Napa Valley Cabernet and Monterey Chardonnay wines with the Gain Bay and Buccio labels. His company, Location, Elevation and Slopes, Inc., is in Petaluma in Sonoma County. Contact him at (707) 971-9636, posert@sbcglobal.net or www.locationelevationslopes.com..

Posert has more than 20 years of experience as a wine professional. He worked for major wineries in California (Sutter Home and Chateau St. Jean) and in Oregon (Elk Cove and Chateau Benoit). Prior to working at the wineries, he was a retailer in San Francisco Bay Area where his love of wine began. His commentary on wine has been featured in print, radio and television, and he has been a featured speaker in seminars and wine trade shows around the country and a past president of the Oregon Wine Marketing Council.

Promoting Mendocino County's Wines
Paige Poulos

It was 2008. Mendocino County, just north of Sonoma and Napa County wine regions, was ready to step out and refocus trade and consumer market attention on its outstanding wines and diversity of appellations. My agency won the account.

The selection committee feedback was interesting: there was the fact that the agency's chief presenter, Paige Poulos, was the fifth generation in a pioneering Mendocino County family; from the first, the agency told the audience, "It will take longer and cost more than you plan to spend to achieve your goals" and this was very much appreciated by the leadership of the organization, who knew it was true but seldom acknowledged in agency presentations; there was a diversity of broad strokes ideas to be explored if the agency was selected; and there was an impressive 18-year track record of agency success.

Among the many programs ultimately implemented, the following three are representative of the challenges and opportunities:

- Development of a unifying slogan
- Educate the local community and set the stage for a book about the region
- Wines for Charity

A unifying slogan for the Mendocino County wine region

The launch of a new slogan is not to be taken lightly, especially in this era of instantly accessible permanent public access to information. Any slogan advanced is, in essence, forever in the ether. For a wine region, it must speak for the entire winegrower community; it must appeal to the wine lover as well as the traveler making a destination decision; it must have a bedrock integrity —be obviously true —and it must strike some enduring chord in the market.

The great trend of the 21st century is the awakening of consumer consciousness of the value and importance of living as lightly as possible on the planet –being "green" is a concept that most of the world's wine drinking public embraces.

Was it true? Yes. Mendocino County may be the cradle of California's "back to the land movement" of the 1960's. The nation's first organic winery was founded here and remains at the forefront of the organic wine market (Frey Vineyards & Winery); the largest winery solar array was already several years old and far ahead of its time; (Fetzer Vineyards), the nation's first carbon neutral winery with a demonstration wetlands and innovative green marketing programs (Parducci Winery) was experiencing strong sales growth; and the newest winery was a model for water reclamation and recycling (Jim Ball).

What attracted visitors? Polls showed that beyond the obvious lure of beautiful wine tasting rooms with excellent wines, tourists were attracted to the wildness of the untamed coastline and millions of acres of wilderness and diversity of local, regional, state and national parks and forests. They liked to hike, bike, boat, hunt, fish, ride horses and go birding and whale watching. They loved the fish fresh from the Pacific, the local fruit and vegetables found on restaurant menus together with the area's beef and lamb, all savored with a fine local wine.

And so the slogan emerged from the truth: Mendocino County is "America's Greenest Wine Region."

Educate the local community and set the stage for a book about the region

For decades, savvy wine marketers have shared the "story behind the wine." The passion and inspirations of the winemaker, the dreams of winery owners, the unique qualities of the soil of each vineyard acre, and more. Today, in a time of water rationing and urban sprawl pressure, it is more important than ever for local residents and businesses to know and understand the farming community and have a clear vision of how each community benefits greatly from the presence of a thriving farming and ranching community.

Paige Poulos considered that one of the really great books about Mendocino County wine and food was written by Heidi Cusick (now Heidi Dickerson) some 20 years ago. The book was out of print but still highly regarded; Heidi was very active in the community and had an interest in authoring a new comprehensive tome on the subject, and the local public could benefit from a greater knowledge of the region's vintners and winegrape growers. But a book is an expensive and time consuming undertaking. At Paige Poulos Communications, we had a two- to three-year strategy to get there. We wanted to start sharing stories as soon as possible and within extremely tight budget constraints, support Heidi's research work, create a new wine and food column for the local newspaper, The *Ukiah Daily Journal,* and set the stage for a future book.

It started with the newspaper. At a meeting with Ukiah Daily Journal Editor K.C. Meadows, the idea for a weekly column showcasing one winery each week, with features on each of the county's unique public wine events (Taste of Redwood Valley, The Alsace and Pinot Noir Festivals, Hopland Passport, etc.) was very well-received. Ms. Meadows pledged front page column heading in the Sunday editions, giving space for up to 800 words and several photos. This was an enormously generous and far-sighted decision.

Next, back to Heidi to work out a budget for the weekly column and a contract detailing copyrights, frequency and a framework for a future book deal, and then to the Mendocino Winegrape & Wine Commission Board of Directors for approval. The campaign garnered unanimous support and the first column appeared within a few weeks. Concurrently, PPC syndicated the article to a national wine media audience, with distribution paid for by Visit Mendocino, the county's travel and tourism bureau.

Two years later, the book deal has been struck and the wine columns continue to run, now working their way through the winegrape grower community. It is a tremendous success, with a countywide audience having a better understanding of the industry, its community benefits, and a sense of the families behind the brands. Many wineries and winegrape growers using the articles in their promotional literature. And the annual feature stories on the wine events have increased their profile and attendance numbers. The column appears first in the *Ukiah Daily Journal* and is also archived online at the Mendocino Winegrape & Wine Commission's website, www.mendowine.com. Total budget, from four years of weekly columns to published book: expected to be about $150,000. Value: priceless!

***

President and founder of Paige Poulos Communications, Inc., Paige Marie Poulos spent more than 30 years in wine industry public relations and marketing. In 2010, Poulos left the wine industry to focus her energies on the expansion of California's organic farm community. In 2011 she co-founded John Woolley Ranch Hay Sales, the nation's first hay brokerage devoted exclusively to the sourcing and sales of certified organic hays for dairies and meat producers. She serves on the North Coast Regional Food Systems Advisory Board, is the vice-president of the Mendocino Organic Network, serves on the CDFA's Small Dairy Herd Working Group, and is president of the Grace Hudson Museum Board of Trustees.

AWARE (American Wine Alliance for Research and Education)

Patricia Schneider

In 1989, AWARE was created by vintners, growers, wine retailers and other professionals who were frustrated with the industry's lack of leadership on health and social issues. A national scare on the use of the compound ALAR caused major national airlines to ban the sale and service of wine on its domestic flights. This particular winery and the industry itself were without resources or capability to respond to inaccurate and unwarranted health scare claims. Internally, wine industry officers had stifled any debate or meaningful discussion on these important scientific matters. Wine Institute Health and Social Issues department and research funding was placed on the chopping block with a proposed 50% budget cut and paralysis at Wine Institute overall had set in.

Enter a grassroots network of individuals and groups – with minimal funding and "big heart"– which set out to communicate a simple message about wine's role in society. This was a time when the federal government equated alcohol with illegal drugs and tobacco; tax equalization between wine, beer and spirits was advocated by many; moderation was viewed as an evil term and common sense about drinking practices was abandoned. The first lawsuit on behalf of a woman who had consumed a fifth of spirits daily during her pregnancy and given birth to a child with fetal alcohol effects dominated the news.

AWARE's principals recognized that a balanced view was needed to communicate accurate public health and scientific findings about wine and embarked on a mission to raise awareness of the benefits and detriments of wine consumption.

The development and implementation of AWARE is a "David and Goliath" story and fascinating public relations exercise. As its founding director, I am pleased to offer some observations on key learnings as they apply to industry communications programs. The first realization underscores the importance of continuing financial support for medical and scientific research. Wine Institute had hosted medical symposia for over 20 years before sharply reducing and proposing to eliminate this area.

Unwarranted and inaccurate scientific reports can only be addressed by credible social and medical research.

Second, these scientific and medical research findings can most credibly be delivered by public health professionals, not the industry itself. Third-party endorsement of any medical or health claims is a critical part of earning credibility with the industry's diverse publics including media, scientific community, consumers and the trade.

An independent Scientific-Medical Advisory Board of physicians and scientists who could rapidly assess and respond on public health concerns should be established and supported on an on-going basis.

The development of AWARE'S Scientific-Medical Advisory Board was a key point of differentiation between AWARE and any industry trade association or association sponsored group. Led by Keith Marton, M.D., physicians and scientists provided needed expertise and volunteered their time without compensation.

Third, a mechanism is needed for rapid analysis and response to health issues and professionals need to be trained to interact with media.

Literature reviews and tracking of research findings on an issues basis is an essential part of any successful communications program.

The support of small and medium size wineries and growers was crucial to AWARE's success. One irony is that while the big wine industry players did not understand AWARE's value at that time, leaders in the distilled spirits industry did. AWARE received a $250,000 grant in recognition of its successful programs from The Century Council.

***

Patricia Schneider is a seasoned public relations professional who weaves together the strategic and creative elements of media relations and publicity to help wine, food and spirits clients accomplish their core business and marketing goals. Skilled at developing brand-based publicity campaigns that engage consumers and inspire long-term relationships, Schneider is recognized for fresh thinking and execution of innovative California wine PR programs that build brands.

She has won numerous honors for her clients, including the 2002 Silver Anvil "Oscar of Public Relations" award by the Public Relations Society of America for leadership with California Milk Advisory Board's "Real California Cheese" campaign. She also placed the "The French Paradox" wine and health story on CBS' 60 Minutes with Morley Safer that sparkled a paradigm shift and nationwide sales growth for red wine.

How a "Confusing Ad" Made Lots of PR Sense
Ed Schwartz

Sometimes public relations works, but sometimes, when your back is up against the wall, you have to bring in the big guns of advertising to do the job. I'm fortunate that I worked as a copywriter for a creative New York City advertising agency before coming west to the wine business, so I still like to do ads for wine clients as a "hobby."

Our firm had a client winery called Chateau Potelle, up in the hills above Napa. A Frenchman, Jean-Noel Formeaux, owned the winery and his wife, Marketta, made the wine in what was then known as "the French style."

One year Chateau Potelle came out with a nice Chardonnay that one might say was elegant (or, if you wish, a bit spare) compared to the fat Chardonnays on the market. Wine Spectator rated the wine and 88 and said very nice things about the wine. That caused the wine to move through the channels nicely.

A couple of weeks later, Robert Parker reviewed the very same wine. He gave this wine a 67 and I can't remember ever seeing a lower score. The score was bad, but his text was worse—he blasted the "acidic" wine as being without heart, taste or soul. Jean-Noel was sick about it, especially when the wines started coming back the distributors.

He asked me what to do and, like all of us, I was struck by the enormous disparity between the Wine Spectator 88 point score and Robert Parker's 67 point score. So, I thought about it and the strange business suggested an ad.

The headline stated—"Read This and Get Confused." The body of the ad was divided into two sides; one side had the entire *Wine Spectator* review and point score and the other side the entire Parker review and score. The copy went on to say to wine lovers that just looking at what critics say about a wine could often be confusing and at odds. The best way to judge wine is for the reader to taste wine and judge for oneself.

For some reason, the ad's message took off way beyond any expectation, especially in gaining positive press. Jerry Mead chipped in first with a big story calling it "the wine ad of the year, or any year." Associated Press wrote a major story on it that appeared everywhere, also USA Today. Finally, the New York Times wrote up the controversy, using the ad itself as an illustration and so big that one could read the type.

The ad also got Mr. Parker's attention as well as his goat. But I tried to get across to him that I was a great admirer of his, but the ad wasn't against him, especially because I simply had set down the two comments, side-by-side in their entireties.

The controversy went on for months. Nothing has changed since then. Scores still are kings, but it is a good story, especially when a client's wine gets diverse scores. It really is a matter of taste, after all.

My Experience with Public Relations
Peter Sichel

I grew up in a European wine merchant's family. I am the fourth generation, from father to son, to go into the family business. The business was largely sourcing bulk wines, blending them and selling them either bottled under our name or under a brand name, or selling them in bulk. The family, however, also had a couple of vineyards along the Rhine and a pressing plant, where sourced grapes were pressed and fermented. In addition the family owned a small negociant business in Bordeaux and an import house in England and a small import company in the United States.

I became familiar, as a child, with the mechanics of the business, living across the courtyard from the office. The covered courtyard was used for barrel storage, and the cellars underneath the houses were used for storage of bulk and bottled wines. There was also a bottling plant and conditioning hall.

Eventually I was apprenticed in our negociant business in Bordeaux in 1939 and worked there until we fled from the Germans in 1940. I came to America and served in the army in WWII. After the war I tried to join the family business, but realized that it was sales and not marketing driven, so I spent the next fourteen years working for the U. S. Government, ultimately as a senior CIA Officer.

In 1959 the old generation wanted to retire and I took over the business. I first became president of the U. S. import company, but soon realized that a small company had neither the financial or human resources to make a dent in the U. S. market. I also analyzed our business and soon realized that we only had one asset: the Blue Nun label. This label had been developed in England in the late twenties to facilitate the sale of German wines. When I took over the business we were selling seven different wines under the Blue Nun label at various price points, trying to span the different tastes of German wines. We were selling at that stage six thousand cases in the U. S., about 10,000 in England and another 10,000 worldwide. In addition we sold other German and French wines.

I was lucky to find an American importer, Schieffelin & Co, willing to market our wines, so I ceased our import operation and moved into Schieffelin to help them market our wines. The first thing we did was to eliminate six of the Blue Nun items and leave the Blue Nun label, modernized and simplified, on one wine only. The next move was for me to become Mr. German Wine. Whereas Blue Nun was a popular wine selling initially at around $3.99 a bottle and ultimately between $4.99 and $5.99, I set about arranging wine tastings of Germany's finest wines, associating myself and Blue Nun with Germany's finest.

I gave wine tastings explaining the intricacies of German wine legislation to various groups, such as the Wine & Food Society, the Society of Wine Educators and ultimately the Wine Experience. At each of these tastings only Germany's finest wines were poured. We celebrated the Sichel companies' 125th birthday with a "Tasting of the Century" in New York, Chicago, San Francisco, Toronto and London, with the greatest collection of Beeren and Trockenbeeren Auslese ever assembled. All the time, we poured Blue Nun as the reception wine, showing that Blue Nun had the basic German fruity, light and pleasant taste.

I became the key member of the German Committee of the National Association of Alcoholic Importers, a spokesman of the German wine industry, appearing at hearings in Washington on such matters as wine labeling. I appeared on TV and radio programs explaining the benefits of drinking low alcohol German wines, of the versatility of German, read Blue Nun, wines which went well with everything, including Chinese food. I brought the standard book on German wines, Frank Schoonmaker's *The Wines of Germany,* up to date, associating my name with his, and promotied the book in the press and on electronic media. I produced a gramophone record with Columbia Records where a young couple asked me questions on wine, which I answered, never missing a chance to mention Blue Nun; the other side of the record had music to drink wine with. We sold better than 100,000 records in this self-liquidating promotion. Finally I wrote a book which was published by Harper and Row called *Which Wine,* a basic consumer guide to wine, and traveled the country appearing on Good Morning America and the Today show, as well as local news shows, bringing various wines including Blue

Nun to the shows, opening the bottles and pouring them and explaining why Blue Nun was unique.

We sold over 60,000 copies of *Which Wine* in hardcover and over 100,000 in paper. It was given free by a fragrance company for any purchase over $25, and I promoted the product and the book in Dallas and Los Angeles at Neiman Marcus, both in the store as well as at a large wine tasting to kick off the promotion.

In due course the sales increased to a level where we were able to add to the PR effort a great deal of advertising and other promotions. We ultimately sold 1,250,000 cases of Blue Nun in the United States, 100,000 cases in Canada and over 2,000,000 cases worldwide. The initial effort was to make wine choice simple and to use me as the spokesman to spread the gospel. Ultimately the market changed, and my partners were not willing to make the investment to adjust to the change.

It was great fun spreading the message. Even today I meet a lot of people whose first experience with wine was Blue Nun and they associate it with the fun of their youth.

***

Peter Sichel, a fourth generation wine grower and wine merchant is one of the worlds foremost wine authorities, with a specialty in German and Bordeaux wines. He is and has been associated with most of the major international wine societies and competitions. He was a senior official in the CIA and was awarded the U. S. Distinguished Intelligence Medal. The German Government awarded him the Order of Merit First Class for his contributions to U. S. and German relations and he recently was awarded the Merite Agricole by the French Government for his contribution to French Agriculture. He served as a U. S. Foreign Service Officer as Consul in Hong Kong in the fifties. Email pmfsichel@aol.com.

Community Outreach "Napa Valley Vintners' Style"
Anne Steinhauer

I've never been a fan about talking about something without substance and that's what drew me to working for the Napa Valley Vintners (NVV). We don't just talk, we actually do. The groups has given over $100 million to local community non-profit organizations, 75 percent of our local public schools enjoy the support that comes with partnering with a winery, and vintners and growers of Napa County engage in some of the most sustainable farming practices in the world. With results like these it is a joy to share our knowledge, expertise and experience!

The NVV has a robust community outreach program that was developed after two polls conducted in 2004 and 2006 showed that a majority of locals are disengaged from and felt disconnected from the wine industry. In response the NVV created the member driven Community Outreach Committee to provide information and education to the public on the work of the NVV. The goals of Community Outreach Committee are to:

- Convey the Napa Valley wine industry's key messages,
- Develop effective methods for reaching target audiences,
- Highlight the leadership of NVV members on community giving and sustainability,
- Demonstrate the industry's tremendous positive economic impact on the local community,
- Strengthen ties to local, state and federal policy makers.

As such the committee oversees the following programs:

- Adopt-a-School
- Afternoon in the Vineyards (with Napa Valley Grapegrowers)
- Napa Neighbor Program
- Local Leader Tour
- Community Mixer

Each program is specifically designed to benefit the community and to increase our "touch" to locals. We have found that when community members are directly affected by our programming, positive impressions of the local wine industry increase exponentially.

Adopt-a-School

The NVV partnered with the Napa County Office of Education in the late 1990's to institute the nationwide Adopt-a-School program. The resulting relationship between the 37 vintners and their partner schools has proven to be a wonderful combination of financial and non-financial support, creating goodwill and long-term friendships between vintners, staff and students. The program also has the added benefit of connecting the number one economic driver in Napa County, the wine industry, with the number two employer, the local public school system.

Afternoon in the Vineyards

An annual program, hosted in partnership with the Napa Valley Grapegrowers, Afternoon in the Vineyards has become a cornerstone of our community outreach program.

Local vintners and grape growers partner with host sites throughout the valley, opening these sites to the public and providing the opportunity for local residents and neighbors to visit, ask questions, learn about farming practices and share a glass of wine together.

In 2011, 68,000 postcards were sent to every mail box in Napa County and over 1,000 residents visited five sites located throughout the Valley. The visitors left having a better understanding of the connection between the land and the glass of wine they were enjoying.

Napa Neighbor

A simple and innovative program, Napa Neighbor has great potential for positive results. Through Napa Neighbor, today over 150 member wineries offer some sort of discount to local residents (the list can be found at www.napavintners.com). The program allows local residents to feel a part of the vintner community by seeing first-hand what the wine industry is about and helps create personal connections between community members and wineries.

Local Leader Tour and Community Mixer

To facilitate an ongoing dialogue and strengthen personal relationships between NVV members, community leaders and policy makers, two times a year, the NVV hosts local officials, community and business leaders and local news media on a Local Leader Tour. The object of the event is to educate the group, build awareness of key issues facing vintners and growers, and network with decision makers. Topics are addressed using local wineries and vineyards as sites and NVV members as spokespeople. Past Local Leader Tours have focused on the European Grapevine Moth, wine industry economics and sustainable farming.

Auction Napa Valley

In addition to focusing specifically on outreach to the community via programming through the Community Outreach Committee, the NVV also has a program to build pride in the annual community fundraiser Auction Napa Valley (ANV). Under the auspices of the ANV steering committee, the Pride Committee - consisting of vintner, beneficiary grant recipients and community members - focuses efforts on strengthening connections between our community and the positive benefit of our grant-giving program.

In 2011, promotion of ANV giving expanded to include local banners and the production of a video following a local vintner throughout the valley as he expounded on the virtues of ANV funding.

Getting the Word Out

While the NVV has incredible programming to create a stronger relationship with the local community, the effectiveness of the programs is dependent on getting the word out. According to research conducted by the NVV, a majority of residents receive their news via word of mouth, followed by the local paper. As such the NVV focuses outreach efforts in the follow manner.

Whenever possible the NVV promotes vintners as the spokespeople for programming. For example, in developing a community video promoting ANV, the NVV tapped vintner Judd Finkelstein, whose quirky sense of humor was able to connect the NVV with an audience that had not previously been reached. In the video, Judd is seen educating people at classic

Napa Valley establishments including Buttercream Bakery, Calistoga Spa, and American Canyon High School on the positive aspects of Auction giving. In like manner, the NVV also relies on vintners to engage with the public, enabling the community to connect directly with their vintner neighbors.

Additional outreach efforts include public relations and local advertising.

Public relations efforts include:

- Working with reporters in developing articles
- Drafting op-eds and letters to the editor
- Posting on Facebook, Twitter and blog pages
- Utilizing the NVV Vintner Quarterly, an electronic community newsletter

The NVV uses local advertisements to promote and thank volunteers for Auction Napa Valley and share wineries participating in the Napa Neighbor and Napa Green programs. We have found that local advertising increases not only community awareness of programs but winery participation as well.

Results

Over the years NVV's community outreach program has grown from a small idea in to a far-reaching effort. It is becoming clear that as a community we are connected and dependent on one another to continue to promote, protect and enhance the Napa Valley as a premier global wine growing region.

***

Anne Steinhauer is the Community Relations Manager for the Napa Valley Vintners. Steinhauer is charged with all community outreach, sustainable farming and winery practices and some industry issues work. She is a graduate of Leadership Napa Valley (Class 23) and currently sits on the Board of Directors for the Calistoga Chamber of Commerce. Steinhauer was raised in St. Helena and after spending some time in Washington DC, currently resides in Calistoga. To contact, please call 707-968-4206 or ASteinhauer@napavintners.com.

Establishing Leadership for Antinori Wines in the United States

Margaret Stern as told to Saralie Slonsky

Margaret Stern was responsible for Marchesi Antinori public relations in the U.S. for over 20 years. Saralie Slonsky, a seasoned wine and food public relations executive, uses the following Antinori case history in her New York University class to demonstrate the effective use of public relations in differentiating and building a brand.

Marchesi Antinori, a wine producer in Italy for over 600 years, decided in March 1987 to establish a significant presence for its wines in the United States. Antinori wines had been imported in the U.S. for over a century, but there had been limited promotional support. Worse, at this time the image of Italian wine in the U.S. was decidedly downscale due in large part to the thin, acidic, cheap Chianti popular in "spaghetti joints," a phenomenon created by G.I.'s nostalgic memories of the Chianti they drank in Italy during World War II, memories kindled by the wine's traditional straw-wrapped *fiasco* that was more appreciated for its 'artsy' image as a candle-holder than for the wine in the bottle.

Ergo, in American minds, Italian wines were cheap, mass produced and barely a step above California jug "Chiantis." This was still the time when snob appeal was critical, certainly as important to sales in America as taste; and French wines were the only ones with desirable image. As a result, even though the straw Chianti *fiasco* was rapidly disappearing and the wines improving, Italian wines continued to be ignored on the wine lists of America's finest restaurants, nor were they served in non-Italian homes; in fact, their reputation was summarized in one word, "plonk."

Clearly, this was not an environment in which an Italian wine brand could grow. So Piero Antinori, head of the Marchesi Antinori family and firm, called a meeting with his importer's president, vice president of marketing and of public relations, Margaret Stern, new to the company. He stated that his objective was to increase sales by 22 percent each of the next five years.

The four discussed possible promotional ideas, including the obvious, advertising.

However, alcoholic beverage advertising at the time was severely circumscribed by law, and, as well, Stern said that public relations could be far more effective in shaping wines' images, because strategically-crafted, real and apparent third-party editorial endorsements were far more convincing than advertising. Also, public relations offered the flexibility of targeting smaller key audiences with fewer dollars. Antinori was not convinced. He stated that previous publicity efforts had been based on his family and its history, that this approach had not increased sales by a single case, that he refused all further interviews, and that if he agreed publicity would have to be based solely on the wines themselves. He said he expected Stern to design a program that would accomplish his goal.

Stern submitted a PR program whose objective was to create positive interest and generate wide-spread trial and usage of Antinori wines – as a line and as individual products — among restaurateurs, retailers, target consumers as well as the importer's sales force, by implementing a strategy of intensive communications designed to demonstrate that:

- Italian wines could be fine (i.e., enhance the overall image of Italian wines as produced with the same exacting standards, and therefore equal in elegance and taste to the world's finest wines).
- Antinori wines were Italy's finest (i.e., create a climate of acceptance and desirability for Antinori wines specifically as the leading example of Italian wines).
- Antinori wines were as good as the world's finest (i.e., as good as French wines).

Her tactics were simple and easily outlined: participation in showcase tastings and seminars for small target audiences, and, most important, an intensive communications campaign. The program stated that the campaign messages would be delivered to target audiences primarily by communicating directly with relevant segments of America's press corps, especially press responsible for 90 percent of the ink and airwaves generated on wine in the U.S. That included wine and gastronomy writers and restaurant reviewers of consumer publications; beverage, restaurant, hotel/club/catering trade publications, business/marketing magazines, Italian press in the U.S., sommeliers and restaurant consultants as well as the importer's field sales force and Antinori's U.S. distributors.

The program stated that the campaign could only be effective if the press kit, factsheets, press releases and brochures contained a mind-numbingly exorbitant amount of provably factual information on every single aspect of each of the 15 wines it then offered: facts on the history of each wine, the uniqueness of its place of origin, of every facet of every slope of every vineyard of every grape and wine and barrel and vinification and aging to the design elements of the label. Her demand for information from Antinori, his daughters and winemaker was voracious; it was so intense and incessant — each response from the vintner prompting Stern to follow up with yet more questions, the five Ws: who/what/where/when/why — that the Antinori clan often teased Stern and, more often, lost patience with her demands for information.

But her fact sheets were legendary, became renowned, probably as much for the fact that they were covered margin to margin in type with barely any white space on the page, as for their detail, thoroughness and eloquence. Antinori complained that no one cared about such detail. Stern agreed, no one could possibly care nor write about all of the facts in each fact sheet but, she asked, how was she to know which writer cared about which fact, so how could she possibly leave any out? She added that the point wasn't for writers to use all or, indeed, any of the information. The point was simply to register that Antinori was a producer of serious wines, for only serious hand-crafted wines could be described in such minute, exacting and excruciating detail. She did not add, though it was well known among America's leading wine writers, that Stern had never met a fact she didn't love.

This tactic was successful, with listings in French restaurants, hundreds of millions of impressions annually, and results as diverse as a 20-page cover spread, "Antinori's Renaissance" in *Wine Spectator* to NBCs Today Show. Piero Antinori became the lightening rod for the "Tuscan Revolution" that ultimately included gastronomy and eventually grew to include the wines, and then the foods, of all of Italy's regions. Not least, sales did grow by over 20 percent, compounded, a year, as Antinori had demanded. And, amusingly for the man who said he wanted publicity only for his wines, not himself, *Wine Spectator's* cover blazoned the subhead "How Tuscany's Visionary Vintner Took Back His Empire," with a full-page photo of the man.

Asked by Slonsky to comment, Stern said, "In public relations, even in this age of technological communications, words, facts and messages are the tools that matter most in building a brand's image."

***

Margaret Stern has been chairman and CEO of The Michael Stern Parkinson's Research Foundation since 2008. Prior to her work in the neurological field, her career was in marketing and public relations. In 1990 she founded Margaret Stern Communications, Inc., to provide specialized communications and marketing programs, primarily for international clients. Prior to founding her own company, she was vice president and director of external affairs/public relations for the Buckingham Wile, Seagram Wine, Wine Spectrum (Coca-Cola) and Schieffelin Companies as well as brand manager at Schieffelin and vice president director of marketing at Frederick Wildman & Sons (Hiram Walker-Allied Vintners).

Blow Drying the Vineyard
Paul Wagner

When it comes to hard news, we who do public relations in the wine industry are often at a disadvantage. The release of a new vintage of Sauvignon Blanc may be exciting to the sales force (or the winemaker's mother), but it is unlikely to make the six o'clock news. Wine is an esoteric enough subject that most of what we find interesting falls beneath the radar of assignment editors and news producers.

The situation gets even more complex when we try to combine the need to generate news coverage with the desire for appropriate content in that coverage. Yes, we could photograph the winemaking staff dancing naked in an empty fermentation tank, but how will that help position the winery as one of the leading grape growers in the Napa Valley?

Our client was, in fact, one of the leading grape growers in the Napa Valley, and we were strongly encouraged to generate more coverage for those vineyards. Some of the best vineyards in California and an innovative approach to grape growing and winemaking made a combination that spoke to both the quality and consistency of the wines.

We tried a number of approaches. We sent samples of the wines with packages of the soil from each vineyard, to emphasize the differences in terroir. We sent both the winemaker and the vineyard manager out on the road to meet media and tell their story of their cooperative efforts. We hosted events, organized presentations at seminars, donated auction lots, and invited wine writers to visit. All of these achieved some results, but none of them created the big bang.

And then one rainy day during harvest, one of my account executives asked me what I thought the impact of the rain might have on the grapes. Knowing that the vineyard manager would have the best perspective, I encouraged her to call him and ask for his point of view.

The vineyard manage told her that the vines would be fine, as long as the water didn't stay too long on the vines. If the weather cleared and there was a good wind, the grapes would still make delicious wine.

Unfortunately, the next day dawned overcast and humid, so she called the vineyard manager again. This time, he was less confident. He was so worried that the moist weather would create rot in the grapes that he had hired a helicopter to fly over the vineyard the next day. The wash from the chopper's rotors would dry out the vineyard and protect the grapes from mold. It was an emergency procedure; one that had been used many times before.

But the media didn't know that. And when one of our staff suggested that the vineyard manager was using a helicopter to "blow dry" the vineyard, we knew we had the makings of a good story.

Our client was skeptical at first. The winery knew it wasn't a new technique and feared it would not be news. And there were worries that it would not put the winery in a positive light. We convinced them by role playing the interview, and giving media training to the vineyard manager to help focus on key messages.

Then we called the stations.

The results were impressive. All four local San Francisco news channels sent crews to the vineyard to film the "blow drying" sequence, and all four used the footage on their primetime news shows. The combination of a "new" technique and a story about how local farmers were reacting to the unusual weather made for good TV news. One network syndicated the story and it appeared in about twenty additional markets. The winery got great placement, and the vineyard manager did a good job of hitting the key copy points during the interviews.

The whole process underscored what we believe are some of the key points to doing good public relations. You have to stay in contact with the client, because if you don't, you may completely miss an opportunity for news placement. You have to be willing to challenge the client to win good coverage for a story. Often, the client isn't the best judge of what is news. You have to prepare your client for the media, to make sure that the key messages come through loud and clear. And you have to be creative about how you package a story. If you do it all right, you just might make the six o'clock news.

There was an additional benefit to this story that went beyond public relations. Two of those news stations sent their own helicopter crews to cover the story. They asked the vineyard manager for advice on how to best film the process. He gave detailed instructions on where and when they should fly. It was only after they took to the air that I realized his strategy.

He wasn't worried about the best camera shot, but he certainly knew how to direct two additional helicopters to dry out his vineyard.

***

Paul Wagner formed Balzac Communications & Marketing in 1991. Clients include a broad range of national and international companies and organizations, with primary focus in the food and beverage industries. He is an instructor and guest lecturer at universities throughout the world on communications, public affairs, wine and wine marketing. With Liz Thach and Janeen Olsen, he authored a book: *Wine Marketing & Sales, Strategies for a Saturated Market* by The Wine Appreciation Guild, which won the Gourmand International Award in 2008 for the best wine book of the year for professionals.

Wagner has judged many national and international wine competitions, is a founding member of the Academy of Wine Communications, a member of the nominations committee of the Culinary Institute of America's Vintner's Hall of Fame, and was inducted into the Spadarini della Castellania di Soave in 2005. In 2009 he was honored with a "Life Dedicated to Wine" award at the Feria Nacional del Vino (FENAVIN) in Spain.

Sonoma Valley Auction and Wine Country Weekend
Lisa Adams Walter

To the outside observer, wine regions and their respective trade associations can appear to be pretty much the same. Each region has wineries and vineyards; each "appellation association" has its role in representing and promoting the region. And when it comes time to develop marketing and public relations strategy, some might just get out the cookie cutter and attempt to replicate another region.

While this approach might be easy to implement, it's not a sustainable strategy if the goal is to achieve growth and recognition for a particular wine appellation.

Having worked in marketing and public relations for several such appellation associations, I have found that these organizations, as well as the regions they represent, are intricately intertwined with the highly-sought wine country lifestyle—the cuisine, culture, entertainment, rural setting, politics and, of course, the wines of the region.

The true challenge is in standing above all of these influences, identifying the qualities that make the region unique and then crafting "the story" to make that region stand apart. Some appellation associations do this quite well and some do not.

I began my career at Inglenook Napa Valley, a winery steeped in history and tradition, and I learned about the importance of "the story" and the impact of that message on the perception of the wine and its region.

Now more than 25 years into my career, I have worked for a number of clients focused on wine, the wine country, food, travel and the arts. One of my many clients was for more than five years the Sonoma Valley Vintners & Growers Alliance, and then recently the newly-formed Sonoma Wine Country Weekend.

The Sonoma Valley Vintners & Growers Alliance (SVVGA) was formed in 1992 by merging the Sonoma Valley Vintners Association and the Sonoma Valley Grape Growers Association. Back in the early '90s, within a year of its formation, the SVVGA created the Sonoma Valley Harvest Wine Auction to raise money for local charities, but also to bring visibility to their wine region. From the start, the auction turned out to be a charity wine event unlike the others. At first it poked fun at other pricey, attitude-ridden wine auctions. Now, nearly two decades later, it has maintained its edgy and somewhat casual approach while maturing into a serious, yet hip, world-class charity wine event.

The Sonoma Wine Country Weekend is the relatively new charity event created by a collaboration of the SVVGA and the Sonoma County Vintners (SCV). This event now includes the Sonoma Valley Harvest Wine Auction, as well as Taste of Sonoma at MacMurray Ranch, and features vintners and growers from the Sonoma Valley as well as all of the other appellations within the of Sonoma County.

The establishment of the Sonoma Valley Harvest Wine Auction, and now Sonoma Wine Country Weekend, has also been one of the keys to identifying and subsequently capitalizing on several of the important unique features of everything that is so uniquely "Sonoma" – important pieces of the Sonoma "story." In retrospect, one thing is clear—in promoting the Sonoma Valley and now the entire Sonoma County, there has been success in trumpeting uniqueness.

Sonoma Valley, and the entire Sonoma County, isn't Napa, nor Mendocino, Monterey nor Bordeaux. Moreover, Sonoma doesn't want to be anything but Sonoma. Maybe it was due to my outsider's perspective (my family has been in Napa for more than 70 years), but from the start, the wine community in Sonoma did one thing right: created an event that personified the image and story that made them unlike everything and everyone else.

Back to the Sonoma Valley Harvest Wine Auction. Every Labor Day weekend vintners and growers don costumes, come out of their shells, get up on stage with the auctioneer and have a great time raising important funds for local charities. Now, the auction is just one piece of a multi-day premium wine and cuisine affair that features several activities such as winery lunches and barbecues, winery dinner parties, the signature wine and culinary festival known as Taste of Sonoma at MacMurray Ranch, and the quintessential Sonoma Valley Harvest Wine Auction. In 2011 more than 4,000 tickets were sold to a variety of events over the weekend. The wine industry is known to be generous. Monies raised have been donated to charities throughout Sonoma County focused upon health care, education, children, youth services, farmworkers and the environment.

The results? The Sonoma Valley Harvest Wine Auction has been repeatedly listed as one of the top 10 charity wine events in the United States. Sonoma County is repeatedly featured in national and international media and has been even further elevated as a world-class grapegrowing and winemaking region, as well as top-notch wine country destination. Most importantly, though, Sonoma Wine Country Weekend has put millions of dollars into the community, which in turn supports the wine business.

In public relations, at times it can be pretty basic. It's all about finding a way to be unique, communicate that difference, stand out in the crowd and then – using a multitude of creative events and tools – tell the story.

***

Lisa Adams Walter has a diverse professional background spanning more than 20 years that includes PR, promotional marketing and writing experience in the wine / hospitality, entertainment, high-tech, publishing, pro sports and corporate environments. Adams Walter Communications, the agency she founded in 1999, focuses on public relations, social media, promotional marketing, writing and event management primarily in the areas of wine, food and the arts using a broad range of tactics from traditional message development and dissemination, to the latest new media and Web 2.0 outreach techniques. Visit www.adamswalter.com, e-mail lisa@adamswalter.com or call (707) 255-0300 for more information.

Follow Your Instincts: Inniskillin Ice Wine
Donald Ziraldo

The creation and success of Inniskillin Wines in Niagara-On-The-Lake, Ontario, Canada is a story unto itself; but it is Donald Ziraldo's unique public relations style that has captured the attention of world-wide media. Ziraldo is President of Inniskillin Wines. Karl Kaiser, its master winemaker, is a co-founder.

While Karl Kaiser is revered as a world class winemaker, Ziraldo has been referred to as the company's public relations genius. His life and public relations philosophy might be summed up in one statement, "Follow Your Instincts." While seemingly simplistic, this philosophical approach to life and business, most specifically PR, is comprised of many powerful elements that are at the heart of the winery's success. Inniskillin Wines and its famed "Icewine" are considered Canadian household names, and are quickly becoming recognized in major cities throughout the world.

Icewine was originally developed in the cool climate wine regions of Europe: Germany and Austria. Icewine production is ideally suited to Canada's climatic conditions. The grapes are left on the vine well into December and January. The ripe berries are dehydrated through the constant freezing and thawing during these winter conditions.

The elements that make up his PR philosophy include:

- Surrounding oneself with extraordinary professionals
- Listening to the ideas of those professionals
- Willing to attempt the unconventional
- Timing is imperative
- Preparation meets opportunity to create good luck
- Add that personal touch

These elements can best be revealed through looking at Inniskillin's greatest PR accomplishment—winning and executing the Grand Prix d'Honneur for their 1989 Icewine in the 1991 VinExpo International Wine Competition.

In 1989 Ziraldo attended the international wine competition in Bordeaux called VinExpo. He met a young wine representative named Frank Pirronet who worked in France's wine trade. Ziraldo was most impressed by him and so hired him to come work in Canada.

In 1991, Pirronet, now an Inniskillin representative, suggested that Inniskillin enter their Icewine in the next VinExpo Competition taking place that year. Ziraldo agreed and instructed Pirronet to handle the details in getting the Icewine entered into the competition and obtaining a booth at the exhibition.

In 1991, Ziraldo, Pirronet and their team headed for Bordeaux, set up their booth alongside the world's most prestigious wineries, worked the crowd, and made sure the world's wine journalists and wine lovers sampled what was soon to become Canada's national treasure –Icewine.

"We found out that we had won something," Ziraldo says. "We were instructed to attend a ceremony at Citadel D'Or where the grand prizes were being given. We went and learned that we had not only competed against 4100 wines from across the globe but had captured the prestigious Grand Prix d'Honneur Award, the highest award given, for our 1989 Icewine."

At that point he instinctively knew that timing was imperative.

"Immediately I tracked down the representative from the Canadian News Wire Service who had visited our booth," says Ziraldo. "Then I found our PR person in Canada, Jane Holland, and told her that I wanted a release. She told me to get a photo taken."

The idea that "timing is imperative" refers to doing everything it takes to utilize an opportunity when it presents itself, he believes. The second part of this philosophical element is in taking action within a specific window of time.

"If the media cannot get a hold of me immediately, they will call another wine 'source' for an interview or for quotes in an upcoming story. Media folks are on tight deadlines. That's why it is imperative to call them back immediately."

"As the old adage goes...old news is no news," Ziraldo says.

The idea was to create a public relations frenzy around Inniskillin's international achievement. The Canadian News Wire Service sent out the story to Canadian newspapers. At the same time, Ziraldo called Debi Pratt, PR director at the winery, and instructed her to send out the media release with the photo. The aim? To infiltrate the same newspapers with the same story and photos, but with a different story angle.

Ziraldo's aim was to provide the newspapers with two distinctive points of view of the same event. The media was provided with a story about Canada doing well in an international wine competition, and a story about Inniskillin Wines doing well in an international event. One story embraced the entire Canadian wine industry, while the other had Inniskillin stand out as the primary "brand" in that same industry.

"When preparation meets opportunity you get what people refer to as good luck," Ziraldo claims. He was fortunate to have the Japanese pick up on the achievement. "The Japanese believed that if the French thought a wine was great, it must be great!" Ziraldo says. "This blessing from the French and streak of good luck created—overnight –a prosperous Asian market for Inniskillin Icewine."

Today, many Canadian wineries enjoy success in Asian wine markets for their Icewine. However, due to the win at VinExpo, Inniskillin has become Japan's luxury "brand" for Canadian Icewine.

Ziraldo also believes strongly in adding that "personal touch" to all public relations campaigns no matter how small they might seem. Debi Pratt and Donald Ziraldo are always diligent and careful to ensure that all media releases and invitations are personally addressed to guests by Ziraldo and Kaiser personally.

"When I am inviting guests to an event, I always personalize my invitations and address my guests specifically," says Donald. "Why? The wine business is a very personal business, and is all about relationships. It's not called public relations for nothing!"

***

Donald Ziraldo founded Inniskillin Wines in Canada in 1975 with Austrian partner Karl Kaiser. It was the first winery license issued since prohibition in 1929. Inniskillin was instrumental in establishing the move to vitis vinifera grapes in the east and Ziraldo was the founding chairman of the Vintners Quality Alliance (VQA), Canada's Appellation of Origin System.

While Kaiser basically transposed the concept of Icewine from his homeland in Austria, Ziraldo acted as the ambassador to the world for Inniskillin Icewine. He wrote *Anatomy of a Winery*, an educational book based on the tour at Inniskillin. He was co-chairman of the capital campaign to build the $6 million Cool Climate Oenology and Viticulture Institute at Brock University in Niagara, which was named Inniskillin Hall.

Donald Ziraldo returned to the Icewine business in 2010 after selling Inniskillin/Vincor to Constellation Brands. The initial entre back into the business was a very limited release of Reisling Icewine and a was planting of Reisling on the original Inniskillin property in Niagara on the lake to make an organic Icewine.

Additionally Ziraldo took on a grander project to release an Icewine from the Equifera Estate which was owned by Kruger Wine and Spirits located in The Niagara Penninsula. The Equifera communications/PR will be based on "social media"…the new phenomenon which is revolutionizing how the industry sells wine.

The PR Business

Engaging & Managing Agencies – it Takes Two
Rebecca Hopkins

There are fewer investments more scrutinized in PR (or indeed business) than engaging and managing agencies. But no matter budget size, resource, work scope or duration of program, gaining agreement to engage an agency is the easy part – the real work comes in finding and engaging a partner to take your brand message to the world.

So before engaging a PR agency, consider a few strategic questions:

What is the objective of the investing in PR vs. another marketing approach?

Raising brand awareness through the generation of publicity is not always the instant answer to a brand's marketing challenge.

If brand positioning cannot be articulated, PR is probably not the answer as clarity and congruency of messaging must be clear before it can be communicated.

What resource is the business willing to invest and what does that success look like?

Successful PR is grounded in building and maintaining strong and lasting relationships, based on an understanding of mutual business needs and objectives.

None of this occurs instantly and may not be immediately measurable so be clear on what the business expects and manage this accordingly.

Once the above questions have been addressed, consider these tips when recruiting an agency:

Bigger is not always better.

There is little point buying a Rolls Royce when you can only afford to drive a Mini; i.e., better to be a larger brand in a smaller agency as it's all about attention and service.

Unfortunately the additional resources that exist in larger agencies may appeal, but the level of seniority, service and attention paid to your account is likely to be less in a larger scale agency if you are a relatively small account.

One style does not fit all.

Different brands need different types of programs and varying agency types. Specialization in the wine industry is common, and a successful agency is one that specializes and executes above industry standard in the chosen area of specialization. A focused trade relations objective requires an agency with demonstrated experience in this area, which may not necessarily be the biggest or newest agency in the industry.

Consider your budget and ensure your goals are realistic.

Any budget scope given must include activation. Don't let the budget be consumed by retainer unless you specifically negotiate a retainer-only contract where no additional costs are incurred.

While media relations should be part of the program, if there is no funding to execute against, there is nothing to take to your audience! In PR, there will always be unexpected opportunities, so ensure budgets are not overcommitted upfront.

Successful PR is as much about strategic plans as it is about capitalizing on opportunities as they present themselves.

Look for demonstrated experience in the field or at least a solid understanding of industry dynamics.

Beverage alcohol has many restrictions and legalities that cannot be negotiated – great ideas must also be realistically executable (and legal!).

Enquire how ideas are presented.

So many great ideas remain just that as people do not realistically know how to bring the idea to life. Hoping the client buys the idea and figuring out later how to do it simply does not work.

Find a partner with a complementary working style.

Account management synergy is important so observe the dynamics in the agency team. Look for respect across the team members. A good indicator of agency culture is watching how the senior members of teams engage with junior members.

Is the potential account team actively engaged in presentations and discussion?

Much like any relationship, it is times of stress and disagreement that will test the relationship.

Spend the time writing a solid brief or RFP.

A presentation against an RFP will contain only top-line ideas against the potential of the programming that is available.

However RFP's do not replace a solid scope of work, i.e., the working document upon which actual plans will be presented. This is where the final creative direction and actionable plans will be finalized.

Ask for specific examples of contacts within publications or outlets.

Any agency can present a slide with mastheads or publication names, but what sets great agency apart is the ability to give real life example of programs, named contacts or activities that demonstrate the ability to build ideas and relationships. Know they know the network.

As a client

Provide the agency with ample information to understand your business and make strategic recommendations.

Marketing positioning statements and core messaging are mandatory, but sharing sales and category performance history, key competitor analysis and long term sales plans where appropriate help provide context.

Ensure strategy and programs can be interpreted to broader internal stakeholder group.

Great coverage is just that, however long term success relies on remaining a strategic and valuable contributor to the long term success of the business.

Check that what is presented is logical and can be interpreted into language other areas of the business will understand. (e.g., sales, operations, senior executives, etc.)

Gain alignment with internal stakeholders early on strategy and broad objectives.

Ensure everything is based in brand language and measurable goals are set up front. Everything activated through PR must be grounded in brand strategy. Not only does it ensure a more integrated and executable plan, it also helps to prove the value of PR in the broader context of the marketing mix.

Review presented ideas for relevance and resonance.

Put on your editorial hat. Do the agency ideas make sense, are they topical and newsworthy? Just because you think it's relevant does not mean it will resonate with the audience – why should they care?

Do not run at the first sign of trouble!

Divergences in plans or scope are common in all agency engagement, so resist the urge to look to a new partner to fix the issue. Timely and candid conversations with existing partners can bring quick resolution and can help avoid the urge to run. Recruiting and on-boarding a new agency can take a substantially higher amount of time than addressing and resolving misunderstandings with an existing partner.

Make time to check in on the relationship.

While weekly or frequent meetings are necessary to keep projects on track, be sure the broader relationship is healthy - agencies will work harder for you if the dialogue is two way and they feel their input and work is valued. They may also be seeing developments or trends in the industry that may benefit your business.

Be transparent as plans change.

Impacts from bigger business decisions (whether budget, direction or resource related) are easier to navigate when delivered in a timely and transparent manner. No one likes to execute less than agreed to, so timely transparency can be vital tool in helping to rework plans and maintain strong relationships. Successful agencies understand the changing dynamics of business, so engage them in working through necessary revisions to meet objectives.

Give recognition when and where it is due.

Paying for a "service" does not equal the right to assume success. Recognition may be as simple as a timely phone call, thank you email or token of thanks, particularly to the account team working on the business daily. Agencies work harder when they feel their work is appreciated. Don't we all!?

Ending it all

Even in the world of the most successful relationship, change is inevitable. Whether it is a divergence of working styles, areas of specialty, or simply outgrowing one another, when a fresh approach is needed, a few simple tips can help the transition:

End the relationship as graciously as you started.

The way you end an agency relationship says just as much about your management style and company as about the project at hand. Members of either team may end up as future suppliers, partners or employees, and if you are regarded as a fair and equitable partner in the final stages, future business opportunities will more likely be positive. You may also end up on the agency side at some point, so remain engaged, respectful and cooperative.

Ensure handover is sufficient but not extraneous for all.

Time equals money, so respect the agency's time, ensure necessary projects are handed over to the incumbent, and remain fully engaged until the process is complete.

Irreconcilable differences aside, offer to be a reference.

If you were satisfied overall with the relationship and quality of work produced, agree to be included in a "Past Client" roster - every business has different needs and they may well be the perfect fit for another brand.

In summary, engaging and managing agencies is a challenging, time-intensive and yet rewarding part of the PR process. Utilizing skills of negotiation, communication, sound business management and issue resolution are key to ensuring a long and productive working relationship, and above all, shared success for all involved.

***

Rebecca Hopkins is director of public relations for Folio Fine Wine Partners. A native of McLaren Vale, South Australia, Rebecca's love of wine began at the age of 17 when faced with the education choice of podiatry or wine marketing at University of Adelaide. Clearly wine won.

More than 20 years later, and with a career spanning importing, distribution, sales, marketing and PR, today Rebecca resides in San Francisco. She has been Vice President PR and National Events for Constellation Brands, responsible for leading the world's largest premium wine company's consumer brand communication strategies and event marketing programs for the US market.

A lover of all good things vinous, as a student Rebecca put her mind to Champagne and won the CIVC Vin de Champagne award in 1996, and in 2003, was one of a handful of Australians to become a "Dame Chevaliere" in the "Ordre des Coteaux de Champagne," in recognition of her study of, and services to, Champagne and its wines. She also served as a Board Member of Wine Australia's USA Steering Committee, and is an active Board Member of the International Riesling Foundation. Email hopkinswinepr@gmail.com or call 415 218-0445.

How to Get PR Experience
Jan Wells

In the spring of 1971, I was invited by Joseph E. Seagram & Sons, Inc. to join their marketing operations for wine in San Francisco. I could hardly believe my good fortune, as a New Yorker who had yearned to move west. Seagram, then the world's largest distiller, assigned me marketing tasks for various imported wine brands which they owned or controlled, notably Mumm Champagne for which I became product manager.

I came to understand that the huge profits which Seagram made on its whiskies and other spirits helped to underwrite marketing expenses for wine, as well as supporting its fleet of Gulfstream and Falcon jets which we often used to visit the far-flung wineries.
Paul Masson Vineyards, one of the best-selling brands of California wine, was owned by Seagram. In 1978 I became the public relations executive. Unlike many of those whose words appear here. I had zero direct experience in creating publicity, although I had had incidental exposure through my previous work at J. Walter Thompson Company (Seagram was a client). The incidents I discuss below will illustrate how haltingly I trod the pathways of public relations.

100 chefs is 99 chefs too many

For several years around 1980, Mumm Champagne ran magazine ads in France featuring well-known chefs. These were all at least two-star chefs named by the Michelin Guide, and they had a professional organization called the "Maitres Cuisiniers" (Master Chefs).

The chefs who appeared individually in the four-color ads did not *endorse* Mumm Champagne – nothing so crass – but each posed fetchingly in his toque in his restaurant, with a bottle of Cordon Rouge in view, never actually held or even touched by the chef. In short, no clear "hook" for publicity. Seagram decided to curry favor with these important customers (who of course served other superior brands of Champagne in their establishments) by inviting them to travel to San Francisco for a few days, including orientation to Paul Masson. This was a solid and legitimate

183

French connection from the PR perspective in Paul Masson, who immigrated to California in 1879 and founded a winery in the Santa Cruz Mountains.

It was my assignment to organize the hospitality at Paul Masson and to create some news. I kept protesting, "Send me five distinguished chefs but not 100, please!" But the deed had already been done, naturally without contacting the experienced PR staff at Seagram's New York headquarters or the novice working in Saratoga. I must mention that the chefs were traveling with their wives, generally, like their husbands, not speakers of English. *Mon Dieu!*

We were able to press into service the new Paul Masson warehouse in the southwest corner of San Jose, a giant space capable of holding 400,000 cases of wine. There were two railroad sidings within the building. My staff came up with the idea of putting this industrial backdrop to good use. We staged 7 or 8 boxcars indoors, put up stacks of wine cases inside them, and then floodlit them to dramatic effect. Towering alleys of wine pallets stretched into the distance on the warehouse floor. Tables were set up alongside the boxcars, and Narsai David, a well-known chef: caterer and on-air personality in the Bay Area then and now, cooked his deservedly famous lamb barbecue for 250 people (including the hosts and a few local personalities) just outside the warehouse. The servers from his catering staff did the honors. Whatever our French guests may have thought about the rustic wines of northern California, they were extremely polite about our warehouse fantasy overall.

The chefs were happy, but would anyone do an interview? And who among 100? (No commitments had been made by the *maitres,* who like all-star chefs are famously independent and who furthermore were on holiday.)

In the end, we secured one good TV interview from a gracious chef and canny self-promoter who understood that one can build international visibility on television, even from the starting point of a warehouse in San Jose. But, one of 100? I prefer better odds.

The kindness of strangers

My boss at Browne Vintners Company, the Seagram marketing outfit which I joined, organized two orientation trips a year to

Europe on one of the Gulfstream jets (complete with a fetching stewardess and a well-stocked galley); he sent sales, marketing and vineyard management people to expose them for 12-14 days to the outstanding Seagram properties: Barton & Guestier (Bordeaux and Burgundy), Brolio/Ricasoli (Tuscany), Julius Kayser (Germany), Mumm Champagne, etc.

I was designated to be tour escort for several of these luxury trips, where our hosts outdid themselves to impress their American guests. I recall vividly a splendid luncheon in St. Emilion where we were served a delightful smooth-textured meat in a red sauce. Watching the faces of my comrades when the chef announced after the meal that we had just enjoyed eel straight from the river we could see below the dining room was a rare treat!

On one such trip, we were to visit a winery in Verona which Ricasoli had recently contracted to provide the wines of that region. My intrepid group of 12, still recovering from seeing the vast Brolio castle with its 12th-century bulwarks, and from dining in Florence, were snoozing on the bus. In the meticulous months-long advance preparations for the trip, I had never received a street address for the target winery: I only knew that it was Casa Vinicola V.

For whatever reason, we were not being escorted by our host from Ricasoli; he was to meet us at the winery. He had arranged for the bus. Before we departed on the day of the visit, I cross-examined our bus driver as to whether he knew our destination. "Si, si, signore," he kept repeating. (I knew no Italian.)

After what seemed like a lot of driving, we pulled into a winery parking lot. I saw no sign of any kind. The driver approached the reception desk. "Seagram ... Ricasoli ... si. si."

The receptionist was obviously startled to see us, but she apologized and vanished for perhaps 15 minutes. after which a courteous gentleman who did not speak English appeared to escort us. I could translate a bit with my French and Spanish, and of course one winery is not so different from another, but the communication was muted.

Our Ricasoli escort did not appear. and as we toured we saw nothing which would link the winery to Ricasoli: no bottles, labels, posters – nothing.

I kept asking, "Ricasoli?" "Si, si, signore," the escort replied. The winery visit was like any other except for the missing link. At the end, on the winery floor, we saw a huge buffet set out for us, with every sort of beef, poultry, cheese, all splendidly prepared, but still without any Ricasoli wines, although there was plenty of Veronese wine offered.

An older gentleman in semi-formal attire – a professor? A Master of Wine or the equivalent? – joined the group, but still with no English. After lunching very well indeed and a lot of smiles and friendly gestures, we shook hands all around and left, sleeping on our way to Verona.

When we reached our hotel, our escort from Ricasoli, whom I knew well, was in the lobby. As with one breath, we each shouted, "Where were *you?*" Only then did I discover that *every* Veronese winery is "Casa Vinicola V" (for Verona) and that we had stopped miles from our destination.

After discussing this astonishing episode with our host from Ricasoli, we concluded that the winery where we stopped, confronting the abrupt arrival of 13 representatives from mighty Seagram/Ricasoli, and hungry for any business from the United States, called on all their local resources, including a very deft caterer, to show the visitors the best possible time.

Having to call my boss in San Francisco to say that I had escorted a comprehensive tour of the wrong winery was not easy. Ever the gentleman, he neither shouted nor laughed, and he never mentioned it again in my eight remaining years with Browne Vintners, not even in fun, although he was famously witty.

My colleagues from the trip, however, delight in teasing me about it when we get together. I reply, "See how generous (and how adept) we are in receiving visitors to wineries."

Introducing light wine

In the early 80s, wines without alcohol and with reduced alcohol were new in the U.S. market and Seagram competed in both categories. My task was to announce Paul Masson Light Chablis (as we still unblushingly called our basic California white table wine) with 7 percent alcohol.

I had become friendly with Carl Cannon, an established business reporter at the Los Angeles *Times,* who was fond of wine. He had sniffed out the story, and I decided to give him the announcement story exclusively just a few hours before publishing it widely. Just as I had hoped, because the *Times* ran it prominently. the news was picked up nationally. (I had never had such a significant story to offer, but Paul Masson's prominence as a multi-million case, nationally distributed brand gave it weight.)

On the morning of the day the story broke (this was before the internet remember), I was relishing my success in my office in Saratoga, south of San Francisco, when I received a call from the business editor of the San Francisco *Chronicle,* the dominant daily in the city.

This was a gentleman who had never previously been interested in any material we sent him, I believe, because he disdained wineries operating on a very large scale. Of course he was livid that Los Angeles had scooped him (no doubt he had heard from his editor), and we shared a few awkward moments on the phone.

Certainly his staff had received the announcement on the wire service we used, but not early enough for the San Francisco morning edition. Not surprisingly, afterward he was no more receptive to Paul Masson news than he had been before.

Supported by heavy advertising, Paul Masson Light Chablis was initially warmly received by the public. including in our Saratoga visitor center (200.000 visitors a year).

A few months later I was on stage at the Paul Masson Winery, built by Masson himself in the late 1800s, then the site of a ground-breaking series of classical music and jazz concerts during the summer months. As the person in charge of hospitality, I often served as MC for the Saturday and Sunday concerts, at which wine was freely poured during intermission for the audience of 1,100 people.

On this day I proudly announced that the wine of the day was Light Chablis and I was loudly heckled by the audience. Apparently many regular wine drinkers had already discovered that when the alcohol is reduced in a wine, its mouth feel is distinctly less satisfying. Chastened, we chose other wines from Masson's lineup of more than 30 types for future concerts.

***

After a BA at Columbia and five years as an Air Force pilot, Jan Wells, a native of New York City, attended the American Graduate School of International Management (Thunderbird) in Phoenix, intent on a career in international business. He joined J. Walter Thompson Company as an account manager with assignments in New York and Santiago, Chile. He joined Browne Vintners Company. a division of Joseph E. Seagram & Sons, Inc., in San Francisco in 1971, with marketing assignments for California and imported wines. Excluding three years as owner/operator of Hog Heaven Restaurant in San Francisco, he has continued in wine marketing and public relations. Reach him at (650) 366-2507 at Wells Wine Communications in Redwood City, CA.

International Public Relations

Marchesi de' Frescobaldi Wine PR
Tiziana Frescobaldi

In the late eighties public relations in the wine world in Italy had yet to become of key importance. At that time most of Marchesi de' Frescobaldi's communication efforts were oriented to specialized trade people, for example, through tastings and wine fairs and some limited investments in advertising. For press relations we weren't very organized. I know that few among the most famous producers in Italy were better equipped than us, and very seldom had PR professionals.

In the early nineties, a deeper interest in wine and food had begun to rise in the media in all the most important countries. Although my family has been producing wine in Tuscany for 30 generations (700 years), we had not communicated our history and the efforts that we were putting into our wine.

When I first joined the company, after previous experience in journalism in Rome and London, I realized that we needed to improve our skills and develop better media relations. Meanwhile the quality of all our prestigious wines, for example Montesodi from Castello di Nipozzano and Castel Giocondo Brunello di Montalcino, had been growing steadily in the last years.

As a result of all our efforts, we also started to approach the media on a more professional way, communicating our history, our approach as wine growers, and writing and preparing press materials. In 1996 my uncle Vittorio, his brothers Ferdinando and Leonardo, together with COO Giovanni Geddes da Filicaja, decided that PR and marketing were becoming vital for the company. We then decided to hire a PR agency in Italy, in the States and in Germany, to achieve more media coverage.

In 1997 an important event took place in the wine world. Luce, the first wine produced by the Frescobaldi-Mondavi joint venture was presented. We decided to make a splash.

We held an event at Villa I Collazzi, one of the most beautiful villas near Florence, designed by Michelangelo and belonging to close relatives of our family. Five hundred guests were invited from all over the world. Many well-known wine journalists and critics joined us from many countries to celebrate the birth of the new wine that expressed elegance and the essence of the Tuscan terroir of Montalcino with the innovative Californian style. We received excellent press, both print and broadcast. Our Frescobaldi name and the brand benefited greatly.

Of course we were glad for the good results but we realized that we had to continue to enhance Frescobaldi communication by creating new initiatives. We set up a PR program for each member of the family, with each interviewed by the media according to his or her role in the company. For example, Vittorio, the President, talked about important strategic decisions; Leonardo, about overseas markets and commercial strategy; our winemaker Lamberto on viticulture and the style of the wines.

This gave us a lot of media possibilities: the name Frescobaldi could come out on the press more often with many different angles: the history, the family, the wines, the investments in the new estates, the markets, our communications programs, and the Tuscan lifestyle, etc.

Parallel to the ongoing media contacts and the different opportunities, each year we decided to host a special event the first year. F&F, a special Frescobaldi Brunello di Montalcino with packaging designed by famous fashion stylist Gianfranco Ferrè, was presented in four world capitals. The next year a dinner party called *Wine & Stars*, with five hundred people at Castello di Nipozzano with four of the worlds most famous chefs, celebrated the best of the Frescobaldi wines together with the most refined Italian cuisine.

Frescobaldi was now starting to be perceived not only as prestigious producer but also as an innovator in the wine world. The opening of two Frescobaldi Wine Bars at Rome Fiumicino Airport and in the centre of Florence confirmed this aspect. We were now perceived as being more dynamic and market-oriented than we had ever been.

In 2002, the purchase of a 50-percent stake of the world's prestigious estate of Tenuta dell' Ornellaia (together with Robert Mondavi) allowed us to make another step forward towards recognition and visibility, and to be perceived as one of Tuscany's most prestigious producers.

My family feels that despite our long history we still want to be very proactive in the wine world, to allow our wines to grow in quality more than ever and to be ready to face new challenges.

***

Tiziana Frescobaldi is responsible for the press office of Marchesi de' Frescobaldi, her family's company, which began making wine in 1092. She handles communications and public relations for European and overseas markets. With a degree in letters and a specialisation in Florentine Medieval History, she has previously worked as a journalist for the Roman daily "La Repubblica" and for the weekly "The European" based in London. She is passionate about many forms of art, including literature and painting.

Introducing Journalists to Italy's Wine Regions
Marina Thompson

There are many different regions in Italy that make wine, but most American wine lovers know only a few, notably Tuscany and Piedmont. Other regions, however, make excellent wines, often at better prices than the famous regions, and want their share of foreign markets.

Introducing these foreign writers to Italian wine regions is a major part of the work of Thompson International Marketing, my PR agency based in Rome.

We bring groups of writers to Italy on junkets, usually about a week long, to learn about the wines and wineries of the regions, imported and not imported in the US market, making sure the writers get to taste the local foods that complement the region's many unknown wines.

It's worth explaining how and why I started this business to appreciate how it works. I was working as a wine importer in Los Angeles from 1983 to 1989, but in 1988 I saw an economic crisis ahead in the business. I believed that importers would have troubles, and in fact, the downturn hit in 1992.

As I observed the market, however, I saw the need for improved public relations and marketing for wine companies, particularly those from my native Italy. I decided to change careers, so I took courses in marketing and moved to New York. I worked at a graphic designer office and a PR firm to hone my skills, then in 1993 moved back to Italy.

Once back, I met and then married Daniele Cernilli, editor of *Gambero Rosso* until January 2011. In 1995 I started Thompson International Marketing in Rome.

My initial business was to help companies get into the US market. Italians didn't understand how complicated the US market is.

We also launched *Gambero Rosso* in the United States during this time and held numerous press events.

The press trips started in 1997. They came from the need of regional groups to enhance their position in the US and other international markets. The first was the Consorzio del Vino Nobile di Montepulciano, which got a grant from the European Community to promote its products outside the European Union.

We organized two press trips, then followed up with special events in Boston and New York. Journalists who had been on the trips invited friends to these events, and they were very successful.

Ironically, part of my success is that to Italians, I'm perceived as "American," with a straightforward manner, not the Byzantine approach that characterizes so much of Italian business and politics.

Recently I had to slightly change the approach. In fact as initially I involved about a dozen writers from different places, mainly US; now I limit the guests to five, limiting the time from a week to four days. They visit wineries with a knowledgeable, English-speaking guide and translator on a suitable small bus. A typical day includes a visit to one winery in the morning, another at noon, including lunch, a free period in the afternoon, plus another visit at night.

The wineries give tours, emphasizing their strengths but, moreover, explaining their philosophy both in the vineyards and the cellar. This information is usually given while tasting the wines many times with some food offered. Whenever a meal is offered, it can vary from a simple buffet at a winery to a lavish meal, often at an owner's home, always trying to enhance the wines by a perfect food and wine matching using mainly local producers.

In some cases, a regional organization other than a wine association will help sponsor a trip, as the city of Manduria in Puglia has to help promote its Primitivo (Zinfandel) or the Consorzio del Sagrantino di Montefalco.

It remains a challenge to convince some producers to make best use of their time with the writers, maybe shyness or lack of good English skills limit this; still I always try to explain how important is for each of them to be exposed to the international writers who can have a "free minded" approach. With more than 400 visits by writers, there have been hundreds of articles generated about

Italian wines, many that would otherwise remain unknown outside their homes.

***

Marina Thompson heads Thompson International, a PR agency based in Rome. In addition to wine writer tours, the agency runs PR events in Northern Europe, and conducts presentations to the press – and sometimes to the trade in Europe and the US for single or a group of producers who wish to be introduced to the leading wine market in the world. It holds press luncheons in major cities in Italy to assist Italian journalists to rediscover or find more about new wines or new producers. In the most recent years she has been organizing events on a larger scale which included seminars, called "The Roadshow" and more events following the same path. Started in Europe and the US, they will go in Asia in 2011. The firm has also organized symposia, such as one on the Aglianico grape. Her website is: www.thompsonwinemarketing.com.

Introducing Writers to South America
Meghan Redmond Snyder

There's no better way for a writer to learn about the wine from a distant winery or a particular wine region than by visiting in person, but the realities of wine writing are that only large media companies can afford to send their writers on such trips. Even that benefit is further curbed during times of a down economy.

To help writers learn more — and to introduce them to his wineries — importer Alfredo Bartholomaus, founder of Billington Wines, began organizing wine writers' trips to South America in 1999. At that time, South America was an up-and-coming wine region – one that most people had little knowledge about. The trips were held twice a year and provided an opportunity for wine writers from the United States to experience the wines and wineries of South America first hand. I landed my first job in the wine industry in 2002, working at Billington Wines in PR, Marketing and Communications.

In this capacity, I was quickly indoctrinated into the planning process of these trips and before long took the lead – working closely with Alfredo to orchestrate the annual outings. During the course of the typically nine-day trip, the writers visited 12 wineries, six in Chile and six in Argentina. In addition, we always tried to include a little free time for the writers to relax and enjoy the scenery and culture of the country. The wineries that hosted the group during these trips were not only those wineries that Billington represented, but also wineries represented by other importers across the US. All wineries were expected to host the group and to pay an equal portion of the cost of the trip. Each received equal time with the writers as well.

Including wineries that Billington did not represent was a unique feature of Bartholomaus' trip model – a concept that many importers and distributors feared when organizing their own trips. This unique element offered participants a more well-rounded wine experience. It allowed them to compare and contrast the merits of many wineries and also to learn about, and explore, the many sub-regions within each country.

Bartholomaus believed at the time, and even somewhat today, that the general knowledge surrounding South American wines and the reality of the area's quality potential, was not a given. Through these trips, he educated people and increased the US knowledge of South American winemaking. He introduced the press to the high quality wines and advanced technology being used in the top wineries in South America. It was Bartholomaus' goal to not only garner press for his brands, but to promote both Chile and Argentina as unique quality wine-producing regions – regions that should be appreciated and respected in the wine world.

Today both Chile and Argentina are considered top wine-producing countries. Even in recent years, most of the writers who attended these trips have still been surprised at the quality of the wines they have tasted, and at the state-of-the-art technology used to produce them. The trips have resulted in many articles on the wineries and wines of South America. Many trip alumni also contact Bartholomaus, the wineries or me, when they are given an opportunity to do a story on South American wines. This immediate connection is telling of the strong relationships a nine day trip allows people to form with each other. Through planning each trip and sometimes traveling the South American continent with the group, I have developed solid relationships that continue today.

During the trip, writers are flown (typically coach class) to South America. It has always been our belief that the writers' experience, once on the ground south of the border, is first class in every way. Therefore, inviting them to fly coach is reasonable. Participants always had the option to upgrade themselves, but that upgrade was on their dime. The group would typically spend the first portion of the trip in Chile and then take the quick flight over the Andes to enjoy Argentina. During their time in South America, the writers tasted the finished wines, the new releases, the grapes off the vine and even barrel samples. They toured the vineyards and wine-making facilities, met personalities at the wineries and asked questions in a relaxed environment.

Each winery would host one meal for the group. The meals at the winery gave the writers time to mingle with each other and enjoy the wine with the foods that complemented it. This trip allowed the staff and owners of the wineries to interact with the writers and to get an idea, through conversation, of the quality of their product as compared to wines from other parts of the world.

The wineries usually visited in Chile were Montés, Santa Rita, Errázuriz, Veramonte, Casa Lapostolle and Cousiño-Macul. In Argentina, the writers usually had time at Bodega Catena Zapata, Bodegas La Rural, Valentín Bianchi, La Agrícola, Bodega Norton and Escorihuela. These wineries are the same wineries that participated in the first trip and they continued to participate year after year. We also had participation from Bodegas Salentein on occasion. We have taken writers from all types of publications and all corners of the US. As a result, articles have appeared in many newspapers, magazines, wine publications and blogs both nationwide and abroad.

In May of 2009, Billington Wines went out of business. Following this event, Alfredo Bartholomaus was hired by Winebow, Inc., as a brand ambassador. Bartholomaus brought with him his unique perspective on how to get the most success out of media trips. He offered this knowledge and began working with the Winebow PR staff to incorporate South American media trips into their marketing and PR plans. The list of participating wineries has changed but the overall outline of the trip remains similar to the original trip Bartholomaus ran in 1999.

***

Meghan Redmond, became Meghan Snyder through marriage in 2007. Following a short tenure with National Cinema Network, she began her wine career as the Marketing and Communications Manager at Billington Wines in 2002. There she managed all aspects of PR, marketing, sales support, communication and event planning. She also developed a small department staff. In May 2009, Snyder joined Winebow Inc, as the Associate Marketing Manager for Winebow's Argentine Wines portfolio. Later that year she also began a freelance endeavor, launching Meghan Snyder Communications. Snyder is a public relations graduate of the University of Tennessee with more than 11 years experience in marketing and public relations. Reach her at megredmond01@aol.com.

The Tasting Room

Increasing the PR Value of Your Tasting Room
Craig Root

I love tasting rooms. First off, they represent an incredible profit center for your winery. If they were distributors, they would be in the top ten for your winery, and frequently among the top five. In addition, they represent some of the best public relations you can have. If you put an ad in a publication, you're lucky if people remember it for six minutes after they read it. If they have a great time in your tasting room, they remember it for months and years afterwards. I know this fact from working in tasting rooms, and having people say to me, "This is where we first discovered your wines, and we've been drinking them ever since." Or they ask for a specific tour guide by name even though they haven't been in the facility for quite some time.

Next to wine quality, the most important component of the tasting room is the staff. People can go into a Taj Mahal visitor center, receive indifferent service and all your effort and money spent in producing fine wines goes down the drain. They can go into a less than lustrous facility, receive first-rate friendly treatment, and leave with a lasting and positive memory of your wines and winery. When hiring staff, remember that you can teach "wine", but you can't teach "friendly."

Let's explore some key elements of making it a great experience for the tasting room visitors.

1. Lasting positive impression

The first objective is to leave the general public with a lasting positive impression. In their home town store, they may be looking at twenty different chardonnays and remember that at your winery not only did the chardonnay taste great, but that the staff was friendlier and more informative than those at your competitor's winery.

The reason I put lasting impression as a first objective is that frequently people don't buy wine at the tasting room. They are on a bike tour and can't carry it; they have already spent their trip budget elsewhere or they simply don't want to schlepp it back home on the plane.

2. Profit

The second objective is to profit financially from the visitors. I like to see the average amount spent per visitor as high as possible. It may vary based on your average bottle cost but it's a significant number to track.

Let's imagine a truly upbeat visit to your winery. First, is the "vibe" right? I have seen so many situations where the staff and managers dread the busy season and to some degree resent the visitors. If you don't want to relate to the public, seek employment in a business that doesn't require a lot of public interaction.

Keep in mind that I know how stressful the busy season can be. When I started as a tour guide at Beaulieu Vineyard in the mid-seventies, we were handling over 150,000 visitors per year. It was so overwhelming that we not only had to lock the front doors and post a doorperson to keep the visitor center from overcrowding, we actually had to block off the parking lot as well.

I do lots of mystery auditing of visitor centers and I can usually tell within a few minutes what the "vibe" is. Everyone from the top management to the tasting room manager to the staff has to be aware of how important it is to be "on"—putting out energy in a cheerful, friendly manner.

3. Physical appearance of facility

Are your grounds well kept and attractive? For example, flowers are always a great way to dress up your landscaping.

Is your tasting counter uncluttered and inviting? Are your restrooms neat all day—not just when you open? I used to work in restaurants: one of the ways of judging a new place is to evaluate how the restrooms look when it's busy. Subconsciously, your visitor will notice these features and grade you accordingly. One tip for larger places is to use high school help on busy weekend and summer days. They can not only help with the above tasks but also perform other duties such as stocking, helping customers to their cars with their purchases, and working with shipping. In addition, they can also police the grounds regularly.

Your tasting counter should also try to avoid clutter. As soon as possible, remove empty glasses or brochures that people leave behind from the counter. Keep the amount of promotional material there to a minimum. Visitors are hesitant to approach a counter that is overrun with empty glasses and brochures.

Speaking of tasting counters. do everything you can to eliminate second and third rows of visitors. If you are in the second row, you might as well be in Iowa. If you are in the third row, you might as well be in Siberia. If you are building a new facility, you may wish to consider what I call an "island" counter which has 360 degree access to the customer or use an overflow counter if your room size permits. If you have an existing tasting counter which is accumulating second and third rows, create an overflow counter which can be used as needed in another part of your facility. At the very least, train your staff to come out from behind the counter to pour so that you have more face-to-face interaction with the customer.

4. Visitor relations

We've now set the stage: the physical appearance is inviting and the staff is "on", how do we relate to the visitors? The first and most important task is to greet every person or group within 15 seconds. A simple, "Hi, folks, welcome!" or, "How are you doing today?" with eye contact is sufficient to let them know you are aware of them and have created an inviting atmosphere. When it's busy, the temptation is to let this practice slide. In fact, this is the most important time to acknowledge guests. I can't tell you how many times on mystery audits I've seen people who enter a crowded room, are not greeted and then leave. Your neighboring winery will be more than happy to accommodate their patronage, listening to how they were treated poorly in your facility.

The tasting experience is crucial to your success. People buy what they taste. Change the mix of wines poured and watch your sales of those wines go up. But people also buy based on how the wines were tasted—which, once again, turns the spotlight on the staff. Does your staff ask open-ended questions? If you ask a closed-ended question such as: "Do you like Cabernet?" you have called for a yes or no answer—which does not lead to a dialogue. Open-ended questions do, such as, "What kinds of foods do you like with Cabernet?" or, "What restaurants have you liked since you've been in the area?" or even the simple, "Where are you from?"

These questions break the ice and start a dialogue. The staff members must keep the ball rolling. It's their job to put the energy into the conversation – not the customer's.

Remember: while talking about your wines is most important, let the conversation flow along the path with the most energy and fun for the visitor. It's a great way to increase sales.

As a side note, it's essential that the pourer understands that while most people appreciate conversation with their tasting, some folks don't want it. The pourer should be perceptive enough to tell the difference.

5. The pourer must be informative.

The customer to your left wants the answer to a simple query; the couple to your right wants replies to complex questions about your winemaking techniques. The staff must take the time to educate themselves on their own. More important, management has to take the initiative to inform the staff on an ongoing basis: regular wine tastings, access to printed material of significance, and keeping the staff in the loop on vital information. Make sure this vital part of your operation is always on top of recent events of significance to your winery. Help your staff be informative! Once again, this is ultimately a sales and public relations issue. A pourer who is able to answer a range of questions inspires the customer to purchase more and respect and remember your facility.

Another area of importance is keeping the staff from having a superior or snobby attitude. It's great to be informative but if you do it in a smug way, you turn the customer off. Americans are still intimidated by wine. It's up to the staff to educate the public about wines in general and your wines in particular in such a way that the visitor leaves feeling "talked with"—not "talked at."

6. Staff attitude toward sales

Don't be afraid to pursue suggestive sales. First off, many new tour guides are put off by the word sales. Like a lot of folks, they associate sales with manipulation: a salesperson is someone who talks you into buying a substandard product you don't need. I'm referring to "helpful" sales: the easiest way to make the point with someone is to say: "What do you do the day after you've just seen a great movie?" Chances are the reply will be: "I tell my friends about it."

This is the same attitude to take in the tasting room. For example, "Sir, I see you have five bottles there to buy; if you purchase one more, you qualify for our half case discount which will mean the sixth bottle will be half price." Or when you notice a visitor holding the brochure for your direct mail wine club: "That club is a lot of fun—we do some great special events for club members and if you sign up today, all your purchases, wine or non-wine, will be 20 percent off." None of these examples were hard sell. They were all made to enhance the visitor's experience at the winery and at home.

It's important to achieve three goals with visitors (when possible):

First, you would like to sell them some wine. Second, you would like to sign them up in the wine club. Third, you would like to capture their email information.

7. Wine Clubs

Since I have broached the topic of wine clubs, you cannot stress the importance of the club enough. Wine clubs are the backbone of a really successful tasting room, mainly because they operate at one of the highest profit margins in the wine business. A thousand-member wine club which ships six times a year at an average cost of $50 per shipment grosses over $300,000 per year.

In addition, there is a tremendous PR value to them. Many of the club members become very vocal ambassadors for your winery and tasting room. What's more, they share the wine with friends, neighbors, colleagues, and relatives in a convivial environment. Lastly, they are paying you to be reminded about your brand, and new releases or varietals. If you receive a free sample of coffee or cereal with your Sunday paper, someone spent a lot of money to get that product into your house. Here, the consumer is paying for this exposure.

I want to emphasize that these clubs are not a hustle. If the club members come home from a hard day at work and find a two-pack from their favorite winery, it makes them happy. So it is a win-win proposition.

8. A full-service staff

People frequently ask, "Where's a good place to eat tonight?" Make a recommendation (particularly of restaurants which carry your product) and then, if the customers express interest in a place, offer to make reservations for them. This gesture impresses the visitor and if you identify yourself when making the reservation, it impresses the restaurant which keeps your wine on their list – or helps get your wine put onto their list. Be a full-service person for them and they will buy more and recommend your winery to their friends.

Frequently, whole families come to wineries. Be sensitive to the needs of children and seniors. If they are bored, they will likely try to get the rest of the group to leave. Have coloring books and white (non-staining) grape juice for the kids. Direct seniors who do not wish to taste to your historical display or antique wine equipment collection. Make sure you have a place for these two groups to sit when their legs get tired.

9. Wine selection

A very important area to consider is the selection of wines you pour and how you pour them. First, try to have a mix of wines that will appeal to your customers. America talks dry but drinks slightly sweet. Try to have one wine that fits that category such as a two percent residual Riesling. But make sure that you also have a Chardonnay, Cabernet, or other high-end varietals for the more knowledgeable crowd. Cater to the more informed guests by opening something special or pour a taste of something not normally tasted that was left over with a trade buyer that morning.

It's good to be generous with the number of wines you pour, but don't overdo it. Six to eight different wines is the limit of what most people can remember.

Change your mix of wine to reflect the seasonal changes in the type of visitor who comes to your winery. The June through August crowd can be different in wine appreciation and selection from the crush crowd—which can also differ from the January through March visitors. That's why it's critical that the manager spend time on the floor so that he or she can assess these changes as they happen and vary the mix of wines accordingly.

10. Responsible service

You are serving an alcoholic beverage; your staff needs to have prior training on how to deal with intoxicated and possibly obnoxious behavior. In many cases, your state ABC will be happy to offer your staff a meeting on this topic.

11. Tours

The most under-rated part of the visitor center is the tour operation. In essence, you have visitors saying, "I'm willing to give you 30 minutes of my precious vacation or weekend time to listen to your story, your infomercial."

Many wineries respond: "No, we don't do tours," or, "We only offer tours at 11 and 3," or, "All we have is our in-depth one-hour tour."

Other industries would love to have this direct interaction with the consumer, and yet we frequently turn them down or force them into schedules which are for our convenience – not theirs –despite the fact that those who go on tours traditionally buy more products and join wine clubs at a higher rate. I recommend that you use a three-tiered system for tours:

a. A 15-minute mini-tour. You condense the half hour tour by bypassing crushing and fermenting and focus on grapevines and barrel aging. If you don't have vines nearby, plant one in a barrel by your visitor center. We're jaded but for a lot of visitors actually seeing a Chardonnay vine is really fun. Some tour guides will balk at doing the mini-tour with, "I can't condense my tour." I find that unacceptable. I'm just asking you to focus on viticulture and barrel aging instead of the usual half-hour tour.

The great advantage of the mini-tour is that it can usually be given at the drop of a hat. People are genuinely impressed when they ask about a tour and you say: "I can give you a tour right now." Remember, the staff member will only be off the floor fifteen minutes. Keep in mind that this technique requires that you have adequate staff. I frequently find tasting rooms understaffed, which is bad for sales and bad for the PR element of your facility.

Also, when your tasting room is overcrowded, the mini-tour is a wonderful safety valve. Thirty to fifty percent of the people in the room will go if it is described in an engaging fashion. I've trained wineries who only have a staff of two to do the mini-tour and it does work.

b. Half-hour tour given as often as possible. A thirty-minute tour gives a more complete view of your winery and its techniques. Also, it is about all the average visitor is ready for.

c. In-depth tour by appointment only. These tours can vary from one to three hours and include food and wine pairing as well. One note of caution: don't pad the in-depth tour with trivia to make it last longer. Keep in mind the idea with any of these three types of tours is to follow the old adage about any art form: it both entertains and enlightens. One excellent way to achieve this goal is to pepper your tour with analogies. Compare these two statements: "Barrel aging adds flavor to the wine" with "Barrel aging is kind of like using a cinnamon stick: it's a piece of wood but it adds flavor to your hot chocolate. Well, it's the same with the oak barrel." Which statement is more easily grasped by the novice wine drinker?

Overall, don't forget to pay attention to your tours. They are one of the most important ways to relate to the consumer. Plus, they increase sales. There are many methods by which I doubled the sales as the manager of the Beaulieu Vineyard tasting room and increased business by 70 percent at Trefethen. In both cases, the tour was one of the keys to these increases.

Never forget the incredible PR value of your tasting room. You are not just selling wine; you are selling memories.

**

Craig Root has over 30 years experience working with tasting rooms: first as staff and successful manager, and then seventeen years as a tasting room consultant. As a consultant, he has helped to create over 60 tasting rooms and 100 wine clubs throughout the US and Canada. He has also analyzed and advised dozens of current operations. He has also worked for other visitor centers nationwide, such as the Kauai Coffee Co. and the Jelly Belly Jelly Bean Factory. Craig teaches and lectures at UC Davis in Tasting Room Design and Management. Website: www.craigroot.com (707) 963-7589. craigaroot@comcast.net

St. Supéry's Smellavision
Michaela Rodeno

Everyone in the U.S. wine business knows that many Americans are terrified by wine. Fear of faux pas, aversion to humiliation by snobby sommeliers, lack of "required" knowledge…all conspire to keep potential wine drinkers from exploring any nascent interest in wine.

When I arrived at St. Supéry late in 1988 after 15 very consumer-oriented years at Domaine Chandon, plans for an elaborate gallery of museum-quality, educational wine exhibits were already in place. I barely had time to deep-six the final exhibit, which mandated to hapless visitors which wines should be served in which specific wine glasses. The penalty for using the wrong glass is too awful to contemplate.

What I proposed in lieu of an intimidating etiquette lesson was some sort of interactive exhibit for visitors to play with. That brought to mind something I'd seen several years earlier: a wine aroma kit produced in France entitled "Le Nez du Vin," which linked hundreds of individual aromas of fruits and flowers and spices, captured in tiny vials, to the wines where they are commonly found. Add that to my longstanding conviction that we humans all come with the same basic equipment (noses, taste buds, memories) that enable us to appreciate and enjoy wine without formal instruction, and you have the genesis of what I thought of as the "sniffer exhibit."

As we worked with the exhibit fabricator to start drawing up plans, another aspect emerged: a visual component to demonstrate that there is no single "right" color for wine. Cabernet can range from brick to ruby to purple; Sauvignon Blanc can be pale green or deep gold or anything in between.

The theme of this wine exhibit was fast becoming "with wine, there is no single 'right' answer." It took us a while longer, and some visitor feedback, to understand that we had stumbled onto something important.

From the moment St. Supéry opened in late 1989, visitors happily pushed the levers that released a whiff of one of four concentrated aromas found in Cabernet (wild cherry, black pepper, green pepper, cedar) or in Sauvignon Blanc (newmown hay, dried wildflowers, grapefruit, green olive). They were delighted to find that they easily recognized the aromas. What kid (of a certain age) doesn't have Proustian total recall of Luden's Wild Cherry Coughdrops?

But the best was yet to come. Leaving that final exhibit, visitors headed for the tasting room. Instead of the usual shyly mumbled "yes," "no," or "I don't know" in response to "Do you like this wine?"; these newly confident tasters started sniffing and swirling and seeking out the varied aromas that they had just discovered to be found in wine. Then they started discussing with some excitement what they were finding in their glass, and voilà –a few more new wine consumers were hooked, uh, born.

As we've traveled the country since, we keep meeting people who have visited St. Supéry eager to tell us that their fondest memory is Smellavision. They not only remember playing with the exhibit and identifying the aromas, Smellavision is indelibly linked in their minds with a happy experience at St. Supéry. They may not even realize that the real probable cause of this powerful memory is their own breakthrough into wine enjoyment. Nonetheless, of all the wineries they visited, ours stands out because of Smellavision. That's a public relations success.

***

During her 15-year tenure as CEO, Michaela Rodeno guided the winery onto the market and through a period of explosive growth. St. Supéry is known for its consumer-friendly marketing approach and excellent quality, and is acknowledged to be the "must see" winery for visitors to the Napa Valley.

Michaela believes in wine as part of America's table and has worked with numerous organizations to further this aim. She co-founded Women for WineSense, serves on the board of Wine Market Council, and has been a director of the Napa Valley Vintners Association as well as chairing its auction in 1998. She also serves as a director and member of the audit committee for Silicon Valley Bank.

A Final Word

Is the Wine Industry "Spinning" Out of Control?
Tim Hanni

I am fascinated how the wine industry has slowly turned seemingly innocent embellishments of increased wine enjoyment into messages and misinformation that now stigmatize traditional, highly prized and perfectly acceptable wine styles and the people who most enjoy those wines. Throw the metaphorical and imaginary concepts of "wine and food matching" into the mix and the subject of wine becomes confusing, contradictory and daunting. One can easily see how a very large segment of would-be wine consumers are put out by the modern tenets defining wine quality originally intended to stimulate and encourage consumption. Today this distorted sense of history and tradition has become the source of the intimidation and overwhelm millions of consumers who associate with wine. And the harder the wine industry pushes the necessity of "educating the consumer," the wider the gap and disconnect becomes.

The Merriam-Webster dictionary defines Public Relations as, "the business of inducing the public to have understanding for and goodwill toward a person, firm, or institution; also: the degree of understanding and goodwill achieved." So let's take a look at the bottom line results of how the wine industry as a whole is doing in terms of inducing and achieving the understanding and goodwill of wine consumers. For context, here is a pair of observations from the top end of the marketing community, spaced 10 years apart, providing interesting commentary and insight on the nature of marketing in the wine industry:

"The fragmented, historically insular (wine) industry generally seems resigned to accepting the wine consumer pool as is rather than aggressively pursuing new markets... the next decade could easily be referred to by future wine historians as the years of missed opportunity." *Brand Week*, May 1, 2000

"Wine market is 'fragmented, confusing, impenetrable'...The wine industry is guilty of going 'out of its way to confuse the consumer', and must urgently come up with 'a new big idea', according to a British advertising heavyweight Sir John Hegarty." *Decanter* Magazine, June 28, 2010.

Since about the 1950s wine marketing has been increasingly portrayed wine as a romantic beverage with natural affinities to fine cuisine. Yet in spite of excellent gains in narrow segments of the global marketplace the wine industry continues to face chronic challenges when it comes to making wine more fun or accessible and less intimidating and overwhelming to most consumers. This is due to simple concepts, such as "sweetness in wine is used to mask flaws," becoming, "sweet wines are flawed – and so are the people who consume them."

I started sampling and learning about wine in earnest in the mid-1960s. I devoured information in the books of the period for many years to come. I was living vicariously through the eyes and palates of the authors and truly mesmerized by the exotic, detailed descriptions of smells, tastes and flavors. Visions of great chateaux, impeccably maintained vineyards and the magical vintages from classic wine regions, replete with descriptions and references to the ubiquitous local foods, danced in my imagination. I loved to explore the regions, seek out the wines I would read about, and apply my ever-expanding culinary skills to creating regional dishes to pair with the wines that were so intimately connected by the people and places.

It did not occur to me until almost 25 years later that most all of the books were written by wine salesmen and that much of the information I had so eagerly soaked up over the years was riddled with inaccuracies, misconceptions and delusions.

Over time, simple marketing messages, intended to differentiate and add value to products as good marketing should, has created an enormous disconnect with reality and history. The result has been a deterioration of information that has resulted in the inappropriate stigmatization of many wines that were once wildly popular and an even more destructive stigmatization and disenfranchisement of the people who drink those styles of wine.

For the most part there was no such thing as "wine and food matching" in France, Italy or elsewhere in Europe. People ate the food of the region and drank the wines there that they could afford. It was often the same wine day in and day out regardless of what meal was served. Sure, there were certain protocols and rituals for wine service at formal meals. But it was clear that many wines we consider dry today were very sweet up until the 1950s, and, in the words of Larousse Gastronomique published in 1938, sweet wines were offered along with the dry red wines, "if the guest prefers." It is also easy to see that sweet wines were much in favor in France, Italy and elsewhere and were typically more expensive and prized than red wines in general.

Post-WWII new technologies in wine production allowing for more stable wine products, combined with the expansion of shipping and global commerce, made wine a great target for development and sales to countries such as the US. The 1950s proved to be a pivotal decade as the *fiasco* of Chianti on the red-checkered tablecloth and idea that dry red wine was best served with the overly generous servings of beef Americans so loved started to be burned into our psyche and became synonymous with class and style. Up to this point sweet wines comprised 80 percent of the wines Americans consumed, albeit there was plenty of cause to associate sweet wines with low quality due to production techniques. This loophole is also responsible for the US Department of Alcohol, Tobacco and Firearms creating a "dessert wine" category – a niche into which many sweet wines have been relegated in spite of the role of sweet wines being welcomed at the table during every course of a formal meal.

This being said, most dry white, rosé and red wines were no less suspect in terms of quality here in the US and elsewhere. The quality of wines was very low in general by today's standards with even great Chateaux and estates churning out, and selling out, wines that would be considered commercially unacceptable by today's standards with fine vintages few and far between. The most interesting thing to note that at this time sweet wines in Europe were very much in fashion, as they have always been, and a quality sweet wine was typically much more expensive than a dry wine. Records show that an estate-grown German Riesling would often be more expensive than a comparable bottle of Chateau Lafite Rothschild!

Going into the sixties the differential between a great wine from Burgundy or Bordeaux and a modest bottle of Rose from Portugal or Liebraumilch from Germany was not all that great. Today there is a vast divide of even hundreds of dollars a bottle. What happened? The wine industry has become hoisted by its own petard. Indifference to consumers who favor sweet or delicate wines that coincides with the emergence of wine public relations run amok. The mission has become to "move consumers up to better (i.e., dry) wines" despite the appropriateness, popularity and high esteem of sweet wines at the table in Europe for centuries. The wine industry cry to "educate consumers" means to provide them with misinformation to substantiate false premises of value and propriety and to learn the limiting and misguided principles of pairing wine and food.

We have spun the stories of wine so long the industry is dizzy with its own myths and imagination and guilty of now perpetuating these myths as inviolable truths. I propose it is time to look more critically at the information we are spinning, reconnect with the consumers who we have disenfranchised with our limiting and self-serving messages, and return to a more inclusive, civilized and consumer-centric approach to the enjoyment of wine: the wine you love is the most confidently enjoyed where and when you feel it is appropriate. It is time to end the "tyranny of the minority" of wine marketers and critics and turn our attention to personalizing every experience and expanding our understanding of wine consumers. That would qualify as a "never been done before" for the wine industry.

***

Tim Hanni MW, a consultant to wine and hospitality business and entrepreneur, is a professionally trained chef. Hanni is a widely recognized leader in developing marketing and education programs that break down barriers that historically hinder the unfettered enjoyment of wine. He is involved in cutting edge sensory and behavioral research projects focused on understanding wine consumer preferences, attitudes and behaviors. Hanni has a unique perspective and passionate curiosity in the worlds of food, wine and sensory sciences. He is known for his modern and innovative approach for creating consumer-centric education programs, products and services. The Wine & Spirits Education Trust in London, England, has adopted Hanni's wine and food principles in their international curriculum and he teaches wine marketing at Sonoma State University. His techniques for creating easy to use wine lists, including the invention of the Progressive Wine List format, and retail wine programs are combined with tried and tested culinary philosophies on "balancing" food and wine flavors and are employed by thousands of restaurants and hotel outlets around the world.

P.O.P. = Print On Demand → Charge more

"Differentiation"

'96 · High Tech Business
- Wine Country
- Winery PR + Marketing

Vitner Good Agency

INTERNET
- Social Media
- Millenials
- Strategic Communications

I-phone
Credit Card

800 in US
NV = 400 Wineries
- High Volume -
- Medium Size -
- CULT Producers
- Tourist Operations
- Attractions

WINE COMPANIES

Price
Labels
Names
Distribution
Tasting Rooms
Wine Clubs
mailing List
Internet = 1% sold

PR = Pouring Samples
Media Relations = Barrel Tasting
Top Score - Robt. Parker
W Spectator
W Advocate

Wine Institute